CHILD DEVELOPMENT AND CARE IN THE EARLY YEARS

SECOND EDITION

Louise Burnham
Penny Tassoni

Photo credits

The Publishers would like to thank the following for permission to reproduce copyright material.

Figure 1.5 © MegWallacePhoto/stock.adobe.com; Figure 3.2 © Andrew O'Callaghan/Hodder Education; Figure 3.3 © Sean Spencer/Alamy Stock Photo; Figure 3.4 © highwaystarz/stock.adobe.com; Figure 3.6 © Leila Cutler/Alamy Stock Photo; Figure 4.1 © Hodder Education/Andrew Callaghan; Figure 4.2 © Hodder Education/Jules Selmes; Figure 5.4 © Christian Horz/stock.adobe.com; Figure 5.6 © Md Saddam Hossin/Alamy Stock Vector; Figure 5.8 © H. Mark Weidman Photography/Alamy Stock Photo; Figure 6.2 © Hodder Education/Jules Selmes 2014; Figure 6.5 *top left* © motortion/stock.adobe.com, *top right* © Axel Bueckert/stock.adobe.com, *bottom left* © Krakenimages.com/stock.adobe.com, *bottom middle* © spaxiax/stock.adobe.com, *bottom right* © Prostock-studio/stock.adobe.com; Figure 6.6 © Creativa Images/stock.adobe.com; Figure 7.2 © Oksana Kuzmina/stock.adobe.com; Figure 7.3 © zilvergolf/stock.adobe.com; Figure 7.4 © andreaobzerova /stock.adobe.com; Figure 8.1 © Hodder Education/Phil Jones

Every effort has been made to trace all copyright holders, but if any have been inadvertently overlooked, the Publishers will be pleased to make the necessary arrangements at the first opportunity.

Although every effort has been made to ensure that website addresses are correct at time of going to press, Hodder Education cannot be held responsible for the content of any website mentioned in this book. It is sometimes possible to find a relocated web page by typing in the address of the home page for a website in the URL window of your browser.

Hachette UK's policy is to use papers that are natural, renewable and recyclable products and made from wood grown in well-managed forests and other controlled sources. The logging and manufacturing processes are expected to conform to the environmental regulations of the country of origin.

Orders: please contact Hachette UK Distribution, Hely Hutchinson Centre, Milton Road, Didcot, Oxfordshire, OX11 7HH. Telephone: +44 (0)1235 827827.
Email education@hachette.co.uk Lines are open from 9 a.m. to 5 p.m., Monday to Friday. You can also order through our website: www.hoddereducation.co.uk

ISBN: 978 1 3983 6880 4

© Louise Burnham and Penny Tassoni 2022

First published in 2017.

This edition published in 2022 by
Hodder Education,
An Hachette UK Company
Carmelite House
50 Victoria Embankment
London EC4Y 0DZ

www.hoddereducation.co.uk

Impression number   10 9 8 7 6 5 4 3 2 1

Year   2026 2025 2024 2023 2022

All rights reserved. Apart from any use permitted under UK copyright law, no part of this publication may be reproduced or transmitted in any form or by any means, electronic or mechanical, including photocopying and recording, or held within any information storage and retrieval system, without permission in writing from the publisher or under licence from the Copyright Licensing Agency Limited. Further details of such licences (for reprographic reproduction) may be obtained from the Copyright Licensing Agency Limited, www.cla.co.uk

Cover photo © Hiroki Obara - stock.adobe.com

Typeset in India by Integra Software Services Pvt., Ltd.

Printed in Italy

A catalogue record for this title is available from the British Library.

CONTENTS

Introduction — 5
How to use this book — 6

1 Child development — 7
1.1 Aspects of holistic development — 7

2 Factors that influence the child's development — 22
2.1 Nature and nurture — 22
2.2 Biological and environmental factors — 25
2.3 Effects of biological and environmental factors — 29
2.4 Transitions — 33
2.5 Support strategies — 39

3 Care routines, play and activities to support the child — 45
3.1 Basic care needs — 45
3.2 Basic care routines and play activities to support the child's development — 51
3.3 The role of the early years practitioner during play activities — 59

4 Early years provision — 67
4.1 Types of early years provision — 67
4.2 The purpose of early years provision — 68
4.3 Types of early years setting — 72
4.4 Variation in early years provision — 74

5 Legislation, policies and procedures in the early years — 80
5.1 Regulatory authority — 80
5.2 Legislation and frameworks which underpin policy and procedure — 81

6 Expectations of the early years practitioner — 116
6.1 Appearance — 116
6.2 Behaviour — 121
6.3 Attendance and punctuality — 131

HOW TO USE THIS BOOK

The following features can be found in this book.

About this content area
A short introduction to the unit.

Extend
Activities designed to increase depth of knowledge and understanding of the topic.

Jargon buster
Definitions of important key terms are provided to help you understand what they mean, and to enhance your vocabulary and understanding.

Check what you know
Activities to help you remember key points.

Test your knowledge
Short questions designed to test knowledge and understanding.

Theory into practice
Real-life scenarios that show how concepts are applied in settings.

Exam-style question
Questions that allow you to apply the knowledge and skills covered in the unit and prepare for the types of questions that will appear in your exam.

Activity
Practical tasks to help you understand an idea and support your learning.

Read and write
Tasks to help you develop literacy skills.

Assignment practice
An activity that allows you to apply the knowledge and skills covered in the unit and prepare for the assignments that you will undertake and be assessed on.

Five things to know …
Provides a summary of ideas or facts that are essential to the topic.

Answers can be found online at **www.hoddereducation.co.uk/vcerts-2022/answers**

6

1 Child development

About this content area

If you want to work with children, you need to know what they can do at different ages. It helps you choose toys and activities. It also means you can spot children who may need more help. In this unit, you will learn how children develop at different ages and in different areas of development.

1.1 Aspects of holistic development
1.1.1 Physical development
1.1.2 Cognitive development
1.1.3 Communication and language development
1.1.4 Social and emotional development

1.1 Aspects of holistic development

Five things to know ...

1. Children are unique. They may develop at different rates.
2. Development is split into four different areas.
3. The areas of development are linked together.
4. If there is a problem with one area of development, it will affect the others.
5. Knowing what a child can do helps with planning activities and resources.

All children are unique. They learn things at different rates, have different interests and also different temperaments. It is always important to remember this when working with individual children. It is one of the reasons why an activity may work with one child but not another.

While children are very different, most follow similar patterns when it comes to their growth and development. People working with children notice their development. They use this information to choose resources and activities. It also helps them know how best to work with children and give advice to parents. Development is split into four different areas: physical; cognitive; communication and language; and social and emotional development.

7

Four areas of development

Physical development means the way in which the body increases in skill and becomes more complex. This is important because it helps children to move and balance and also use their hands.

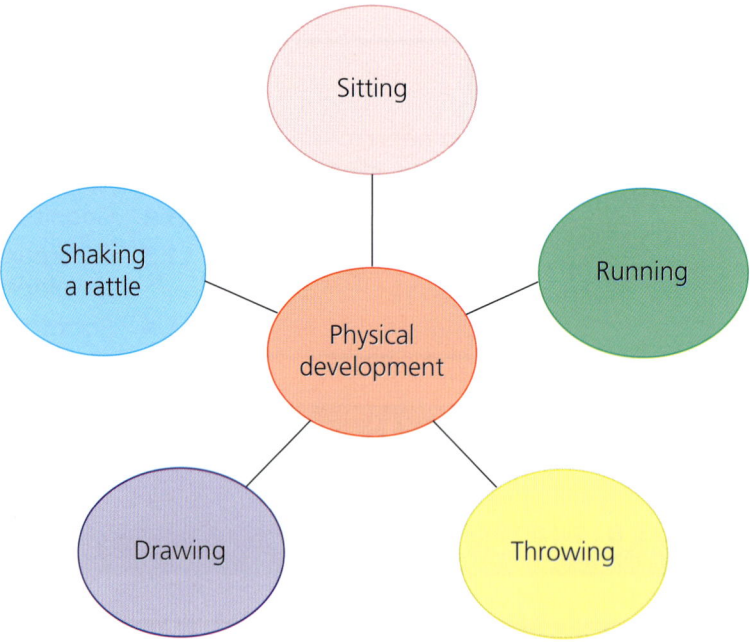

Figure 1.1 Examples of physical development

Cognitive development is about the ability to think, recognise and remember.

This is important because it helps children to remember things and solve problems.

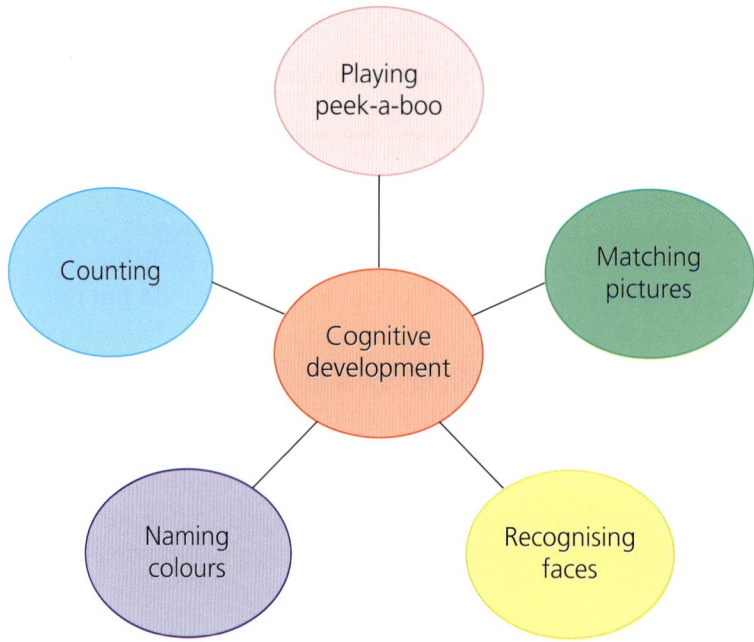

Figure 1.2 Examples of cognitive development

1 Child development

Communication and language development is about the ability to make sounds, talk, understand and interact with others. This is important as it means that children can understand others and also talk to them.

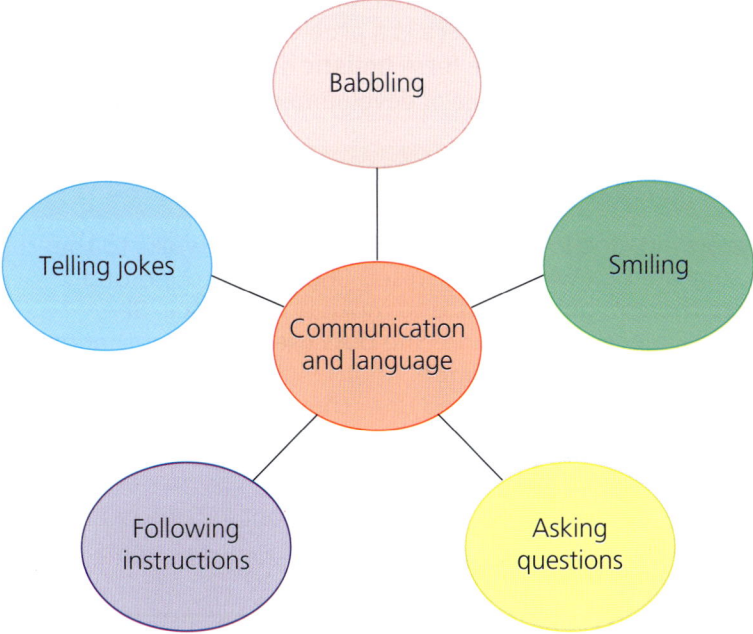

Figure 1.3 Examples of communication and language

Social and emotional development is about the ability to interact with others, develop, manage and express feelings, and become more independent.

This is important because it helps children play with each other and control their feelings.

Figure 1.4 Examples of social and emotional development

> **Check what you know**
>
> Can you list the four different areas of development?

9

Areas of development are interconnected

Each area is different, but they come together – just like every ingredient is important when making a cake. If there is a problem with one area of development, it will affect others. The term **holistic development** is used to explain the way that the different areas of development are interconnected.

Jargon buster

Holistic development: children's overall development.

Milestones: skills that are expected at different ages.

Fine motor skills: co-ordination of small muscles, precise movements and hand–eye co-ordination.

Gross motor skills: skills that involve the large muscles of the arms, legs and torso.

Theory into practice

Greta is four years old. She loves playing with trains. She walks to the shelf and picks up the box with the train set. She looks around and works out where there might be space to make up the track. She takes out the track pieces one by one. She puts the track together and remembers how to make an oval shape. Another child wants to come and play. Greta explains her plans, and later they play together.

1. Identify how Greta used each of the areas of development to help her play.
2. Explain why cognitive development was important in Greta's play.
3. Consider how Greta's play might be affected if she had a difficulty with her physical development.

1.1.1 Physical development

Five things to know ...

Fine motor movements are important for several reasons:
1. They help children to feed and dress themselves.
2. They help children explore and so learn, for example, playing with sand, dough and water.
3. They help children to paint, draw and write.
4. They help children do activities such as cooking, collage and modelling.
5. They help children learn through play, for example, with train sets, play people or building blocks.

Physical development is the growth and skills that help children to move and to use their hands. Most children develop in similar ways. Babies are unable to control their movements, but by the end of the first year, they are usually mobile and able to pick up and hold objects. Over the next few years, they become more skilful.

Some skills are learnt in stages, such as walking. A child needs to sit before they can walk. The term **milestone** is used when children show skills that are important for later development. You will need to know the key milestones and the order or sequence in which they develop.

1 Child development

Physical development is such a big area that it is split into two sections:

- **Fine motor skills** – small movements, usually involving the hands
- **Gross motor skills** – large movements, usually involving the arms and legs.

> **Activity**
>
> Think about what you have been doing in the last hour. Make a list of the fine motor movements that you have used, for example, using a phone. Make a list of gross motor movements that you have used, such as reaching for something.
>
> Have you done anything where both fine and gross motor skills were needed, for example, walking while using a phone?

Fine motor skills

These skills are used to hold and move things, such as playing with a toy car or using a spoon to eat. They are important because they help children become independent.

Table 1.1 Fine motor skills: expected sequence and key milestones

Stage	At the end of this stage, a child will typically:
At birth	■ have their hands firmly closed ■ often fold their thumb under their fingers
One year	■ point using their index finger ■ pass and release toys ■ clasp their hands together ■ hold a crayon with palmar grasp and make random marks
2 years	■ pull apart interlocking toys ■ use pincer grip to pick up small objects ■ draw lines, dots and circles
3 years	■ begin to show a preference for their dominant hand (left or right) ■ fasten a large zip ■ draw a person with a head
4 years	■ begin to fasten buttons ■ use a spoon and fork well to eat ■ draw a figure that resembles a person, showing head, legs and body
5 years	■ use a knife and fork competently ■ thread small beads ■ draw a person with a head, body, arms, legs, nose and mouth

> **Activity**
>
> Look at this photograph:
>
>
>
> **Figure 1.5**
>
> Using the milestone chart (Table 1.1), give the likely age of this child.

> **Check what you know**
>
> At what age can most children use a spoon and fork well?

11

Gross motor skills

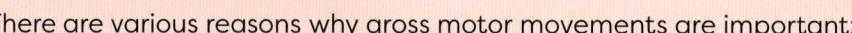

Five things to know …

There are various reasons why gross motor movements are important:
1. They allow children to be independent as they can go and get things themselves.
2. They help children's **spatial awareness**.
3. They help to develop strength and stamina.
4. They help children to play together.
5. They give children confidence.

Jargon buster

Spatial awareness: knowing where your body is in relation to things around you.

These skills are used to help children move their bodies and also to stand and balance. Gross motor movements make use of large muscles in the arms, legs, back and chest. Gross motor development follows a sequence, as Table 1.2 shows. See how the first thing that babies learn to control is their head.

Table 1.2 Gross motor skills: expected sequence and key milestones

Stage	At the end of this stage, a child will typically:
At birth	■ lie on their back with their head to one side ■ let their head lag when pulled to a sitting position
One year	■ stand, and may **cruise** around furniture ■ sit down from standing ■ be more mobile
2 years	■ walk up and down stairs by holding an adult's hand ■ run with control ■ throw and kick a ball
3 years	■ be able to walk backwards and sideways ■ ride and steer a tricycle ■ jump from a low step with both feet together ■ throw a ball overhand and catch a large ball with arms outstretched
4 years	■ stand and run on tiptoe ■ hop ■ change direction while running ■ catch, kick, throw and bounce a ball
5 years	■ skip and move rhythmically to music ■ hop on each foot ■ ride a bicycle with stabilisers

Jargon buster

Cruising: how babies move, walking by holding onto furniture.

1 Child development

Learning to walk

Learning to walk is a significant skill development for babies. It starts with rolling over, then sitting, and then crawling or bottom shuffling. Babies then learn to stand, before taking their first steps. Most babies are walking by 18 months.

Activity

Make a timeline, starting at birth, that shows the sequence of skills developed that lead up to a child aged 5 years being able to hop on each foot.

Read and write

Use ten cards to write ten quiz questions about physical development between birth and 5 years.

Write the answers on the back of the cards.

Try them out with your friends.

Check what you know

At what age can most children ride and steer a tricycle?

Development is holistic

Physical development is important for other areas of development. When development is typical, children can move and touch things. This is important for cognitive development, as it helps children to learn about texture, shape, colour and how things work. When children are moving and touching things, they are also more likely to want to show adults and other children what they are doing; this helps their communication skills and also prompts conversations that may include new words.

Moving and touching things is also important for joining in play with other children. Being able to do things for themselves helps children feel confident.

Exam-style question

1 Which **one** can most two year olds do?
   a Ride a bicycle
   b Run on tiptoe
   c Throw and kick a ball
   d Hop on each foot

NCFE CACHE Level 1/2 Technical Award in Child Development and Care

1.1.2 Cognitive development

Five things to know ...

There are many reasons why cognitive development is important:
1. It helps children make sense of their world.
2. It helps children to remember information.
3. It helps children to make connections between things.
4. It helps children to solve problems.
5. It is important for learning literacy and mathematics.

Cognitive development involves processes in the brain that help us to remember things, organise our ideas and solve problems.

Cognitive development is important in learning. A one year old learns that knocking down a stack of bricks is interesting. When another stack of bricks is built, they knock it down again, because they can remember how to do it. Once children develop language, words help them to remember and think about things even if those things are not in front of them, for example, a four year old saying that they have a favourite colour.

Table 1.3 Cognitive development: expected sequence and key milestones

Stage	At the end of this stage, a child will typically:
At birth	■ turn their head towards bright light ■ like looking at high-contrast patterns, e.g. black and white shapes ■ be startled by sudden noises ■ show **primitive reflexes**: swallowing and sucking, rooting, grasping, stepping ■ have **asymmetric tonic neck** ■ startle (Moro reflex)
One year	■ understand simple instructions such as 'clap hands' ■ imitate and respond to gestures ■ anticipate future routines
2 years	■ understand that a mirror is a reflection ■ begin to understand consequences of their own actions ■ name pictures and objects in a book
3 years	■ recognise objects that are heavy and light ■ show awareness of past and present ■ actively seek answers to questions, and use 'why' ■ sort objects by size and shape

Jargon buster

Primitive reflexes: movements that newborns automatically make.

Asymmetric tonic neck: a reflex where if the baby's head is turned to one side, the knee and arm on the other side bend.

1 Child development

Stage	At the end of this stage, a child will typically:
4 years	- name some colours - count to 10 - recall stories and rhymes - sometimes confuse fantasy and reality
5 years	- give meaning to marks they make and see - count to 20 - understand basic rules - be interested in reading and writing

Activity

Familiarise yourself with these common toys:
- stacking beakers
- jigsaw puzzle
- picture lotto.

Identify the cognitive skills involved in using each toy.

Check what you know

Give an example of a cognitive skill that is typical for a five year old.

True or false: Most two year olds can count to ten.

Development is holistic

Cognitive development is important for other areas of development. When cognitive development is typical, children are able to remember things. This is important in learning to talk, as children have to remember the meanings of words if they are to use them.

Cognitive development is important for learning new physical skills, as children may have to think and problem solve, for example, if they want to use a climbing frame. They may also have to remember how to do physical things such as how to make a rattle work.

Children also need cognitive skills for their social and emotional development. They need to remember faces and then names of people in their lives. As they get older, they need to remember how to behave in different situations. They also need problem-solving skills to think about why another child is sad.

Exam-style question

2 Explain how cognitive development is important for children's holistic development.

NCFE CACHE Level 1/2 Technical Award in Child Development and Care

1.1.3 Communication and language development

Five things to know …

There are many reasons why communication and language are important:
1. It helps children understand what others are saying.
2. It helps children to talk about their needs and feelings.
3. It helps children to play with each other.
4. It is linked to memory and cognitive development.
5. It is important when learning literacy and mathematics.

Communication and language are about the ability to passively understand others, but also to actively communicate with others.

There is a clear sequence as to how children understand and then go on to produce sounds and words. In their first year, babies tune into the language or languages that adults are using. They learn to use smiles and sounds to communicate with adults. Towards the end of the first year, they can understand some words, but while they are babbling, they are not forming words. Babies start to use words from around one year, but only when children are nearly three years old do they start to talk in sentences.

Table 1.4 Communication and language development: expected sequence and key milestones

Stage	At the end of this stage, a child will typically:
At birth	■ recognise their mother's or main carer's voice ■ be unable to hear very soft sounds ■ cry to indicate need
One year	■ babble tunefully, leading to first single spoken words ■ raise tone to gain attention ■ follow simple instructions and understand simple, frequent words
2 years	■ use 50 words or more ■ join two words together ■ refer to themselves by name ■ understand a wide range of words
3 years	■ use 200 words or more ■ constantly ask questions, using 'what, why, who' ■ join in simple rhymes

1 Child development

Stage	At the end of this stage, a child will typically:
4 years	■ be understood easily by others ■ enjoy telling and sharing stories ■ know several nursery rhymes and songs
5 years	■ begin to show signs of reading ■ concentrate and maintain attention ■ use language and gestures to convey meaning ■ use mostly grammatically correct speech

Activity

Look at Table 1.4. Identify the milestones that are about understanding language.

Extend

Visit www.wordsforlife.org.uk

Find out more about how babies learn language in the first year of life and how adults can help them.

Using the information on the website, create a leaflet to help parents find out more about their child's communication and language development.

Check what you know

At what age can most children join two words together?

Development is holistic

Communication and language are important for other areas of development. When development is typical, children can communicate with others, which helps their social and emotional development. When children are able to understand and talk, they can use words to help them remember things, and this helps their cognitive development. Communication and language are also used in learning new physical skills and games where following instructions or listening to advice are important.

Exam-style question

3 At what age are most children using 200 words?
   a 1 year
   b 2 years
   c 3 years
   d 5 years

17

NCFE CACHE Level 1/2 Technical Award in Child Development and Care

1.1.4 Social and emotional development

> **Five things to know ...**
>
> There are several reasons why social and emotional development is important:
> 1. It helps children to build relationships with others.
> 2. It helps children to respond appropriately in different situations.
> 3. It helps children to play with other children.
> 4. It helps children manage their feelings, for example when they lose a game.
> 5. It helps children to cope with setbacks and develop confidence.

Social development is about learning to be with others and knowing how to behave in different situations. Emotional development is about managing feelings and impulses. It is also about confidence and how we understand ourselves. In the early years, social and emotional development are very closely linked.

Social and emotional development starts with the bond or the love that develops between babies and their parents and primary carers in the first year. A strong bond helps babies to trust others and enjoy being with them. Babies need plenty of cuddles, they also need adults who play with them and meet their needs quickly. As babies and toddlers grow, they learn to play and notice others, but become upset if they cannot be close to their parents or primary carers.

At the age of two, most children will have tantrums. This is often because they cannot express their feelings of frustration when they have to wait or they cannot have something. From around three years old, when children are starting to talk well, they find it easier to play with others and cope with their strong emotions. Being with their parents is important, but they can cope with going to a pre-school or childminder if they know the carers well. From four years, children start to develop strong friendships and follow simple rules.

> **Check what you know**
>
> At what age are most children playing with other children?

Table 1.5 Social and emotional development: expected sequence and key milestones

Stage	At the end of this stage, a child will typically:
At birth	■ imitate facial expressions ■ express pleasure at bath time or when being fed ■ enjoy physical touch
One year	■ enjoy playing simple games such as 'peek a boo' ■ cry if unable to see their carer ■ be dependent on others ■ play alone or alongside others happily

1 Child development

Stage	At the end of this stage, a child will typically:
2 years	■ be confident and curious to explore the environment ■ often feel frustrated when unable to express feelings ■ be clingy at times but independent at others
3 years	■ enjoy playing with other children ■ express emotions ■ enjoy imaginative and creative play experiences ■ like to do tasks unaided
4 years	■ welcome and value praise ■ be more confident in new situations and with unfamiliar adults ■ be sensitive to others ■ possibly become fearful as imagination increases
5 years	■ enjoy group play ■ have definite likes and dislikes ■ describe themself in a positive way ■ gain confidence and be more independent

Exam-style question

4 Priti is four years old. She has recently moved to a new pre-school. She is finding it hard to settle in and does not talk to any of the adults. She is very independent and likes to do things without help. She sometimes plays with one or two other children, especially in the home corner.

Consider whether Priti's social and emotional development is typical of four year olds.

Development is holistic

Social and emotional development is important for other areas of development. When it is typical, children are more likely to try out new things and persist for longer. This means that they can learn new physical skills, new words and also new information.

Read and write

Write a leaflet for parents that shows the holistic development they might see when their child is two years old.

Activity

Create a chart that shows the holistic development of children aged four years.

Check what you know

Give an example of why social and emotional development is important.

Exam-style question

5. Harvey is three years old. He is able to ride a bicycle with stabilisers confidently and can throw a ball accurately. He loves scribbling with markers. He loves building towers of blocks, and he orders the blocks by size so that the smallest ones are on top. Harvey is very independent, but not good at playing with other children. He is starting to use the occasional word and mainly communicates by pointing at things.
   a. Using this information, identify the skills that link to the different areas of development.
   b. Identify Harvey's stage of development in each of the areas of development.
   c. Consider Harvey's overall development in relation to typical milestones for his age.

Test your knowledge

1. Explain what is meant by the term 'holistic development'.
2. Give an example of a fine motor skill.
3. At what age are most children able to ride a bicycle with stabilisers?
4. Explain how developing physical skills can help children's confidence.
5. Explain the meaning of 'cognitive development'.
6. At what age are most children using 50 words?
7. Give two reasons why communication and language development is important.
8. At what age are most children starting to play in groups?
9. Give two reasons why social and emotional development is important.
10. Explain how a cooking activity with an adult involves all the areas of development.

1 Child development

Assignment practice

Case study

Amy is two and a half years old and lives with her father and mother.

She has just started nursery and staff are starting to assess her development. They meet with Amy's parents to find out more about what she can do at home. This information will go into Amy's records.

This is what Amy's mother says about Amy:

'Amy is a chatterbox. She constantly asks questions. She points to pictures in books and asks what things are. She is quick to learn new words and will often point out something that we saw and talked about the day before. She is not keen on drawing or painting, but she does like using her brother's Lego® and building models. She loves cuddles, but hates it if I even leave the room and always wants me to do everything with her. I watch other children who go off and explore, but she is like my shadow. Outdoors, she loves playing with a ball and can kick and throw quite well.'

Task

Using the information from Amy's mother, identify Amy's current level of development in each of the four areas of development. Use this information to copy and complete the nursery's record sheet.

Name of child:
Filled in by:
Date:

Physical development	Cognitive development

Communication and language development	Social and emotional development

Areas of development that may need further assessment or support:

2 Factors that influence the child's development

About this content area

In Unit 1 we saw how babies and children typically develop. But there can be differences between children of the same age. This unit will look at the things that can affect children's development. We also look at how changes or transitions in children's lives can affect their development, and how adults can help them.

2.1 Nature and nurture
2.2 Biological and environmental factors
2.3 Effects of biological and environmental factors
2.4 Transitions
   2.4.1 Types of transition
   2.4.2 The impact of transitions on the child's development
2.5 Support strategies

2.1 Nature and nurture

Five things to know ...

1 Everyone develops slightly differently.
2 Nature or what we are born with affects our development.
3 Nurture or what happens to us is also important.
4 There has been a debate about whether nature or nurture is the most important.
5 It is now thought that both nature and nurture are important.

Every child and every one of us is different. Unless you are an identical twin, your face will be different to everyone else's face. Everyone is also different in the way that they think, cope with different situations and also find some things easy, but other things hard. Researchers know that both nature and nurture each play their part in making us unique.

Nature

Before you were born, some of the things that make you who you are were already decided or more likely to happen. These things all fall into the 'nature' category. They include whether you were a premature baby, your eye colour and whether you have or may develop hay fever.

22

2 Factors that influence the child's development

Inherited characteristics

Many things that make us different and fit into the 'nature' category are a result of our **genetic make-up**. When we are conceived, a sperm and egg come together. They each contain information that decides what we look like, our gender and other **inherited characteristics** such as our hair colour. This information is held in 23 pairs of chromosomes. Half the chromosomes will come from the biological father and the other set will come from the biological mother. The key reason why we are all different is that each chromosome contains a variety of genes.

> **Jargon buster**
>
> **Genetic make-up:** chromosomes and genes that contain information to make cells.
>
> **Inherited characteristics:** features that can be traced back to a child's biological family.

Genes contain sets of instructions that affect whether and how cells grow and develop, for example whether or not you have curly hair. Genes are like building blocks. If you have a lot of different blocks, you can build them in a variety of different ways. The same is true for humans. Researchers think that there are at least 100,000 different genes, and this is why each one of us will be different. Unless a child is an identical twin, they will have slightly different genes from their brothers and sisters.

> **Extend**
>
> Visit the following website to find out more about genes:
>
> www.youtube.com/watch?v=5MQdXjRPHmQ
>
> See if you can now explain the role of a gene to someone in your group.

Genetic factors

Genes and chromosomes sometimes change or have missing or extra parts. Researchers are still learning about why this happens.

This can result in health conditions or a child having a disability. Biological parents can sometimes pass gene changes onto their children. This is why some serious health conditions run in families.

Biological influences

As well as our genetic make-up, there are other biological factors that might affect a child before or after they are born. One factor is the mother becoming ill while pregnant, and a disease called rubella (or German measles) can cause blindness and deafness in an unborn baby.

> **Check what you know**
>
> Can you give an example of an inherited characteristic?

23

NCFE CACHE Level 1/2 Technical Award in Child Development and Care

Jargon buster

Environmental influences: aspects of a child's life that will affect their development.

Nurture

The term 'nurture' is used to describe everything about a child's life after they are born. These are the **environmental influences** that will affect how a child grows and develops. They include:

- where and how a child is looked after
- the relationships with people in their lives
- the opportunities they have to do things
- events that might happen to them and their family, such as moving home or the death of a family member.

Which matters most – nature or nurture?

For a long time, people thought that children's characters and development were a result of either nature or nurture, one or the other. You might hear families say things such as 'He's just like his Dad' or 'She's been like that since she was born.'

Today we know that both aspects are at work. For example:

- Puberty: the timing of puberty is partly genetic, but environmental factors such as being overweight or underweight make a difference.
- Language development: children are born ready to learn language, but if they did not hear any language, they would not learn to talk.

The big debate is now about how much of a child's development and personality is nature and how much is a result of nurture.

Activity

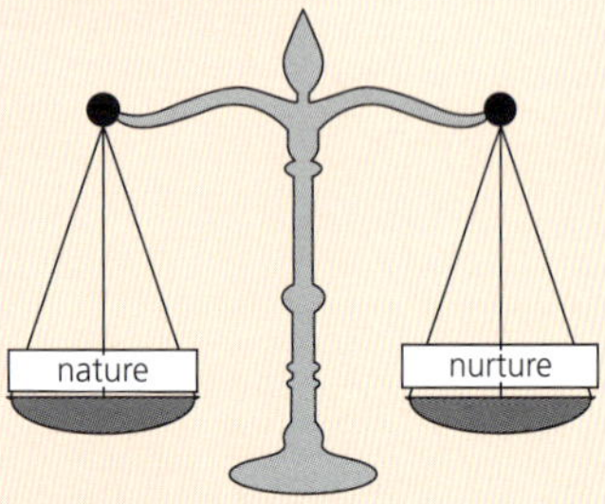

Figure 2.1 Nature vs nurture – which is the most important?

Ask ten people the following question:

- Out of a hundred, what score would you give to nurture being more important than nature in a child's development?

Present the results in the form of a bar chart.

Theory into practice

Rufus is five years old. He is much shorter than other children of his age. His parents are also short. Rufus was diagnosed with asthma when he was three. As a result, he often has chest infections in the winter months. This has meant that he has missed many sessions when in nursery and in his first term at school. Rufus' early literacy skills have been affected. His teacher carried out an assessment at the end of the reception year. He is not showing expected development in literacy. His mother also says that teachers and adults tend to expect less of him because he looks much younger than he really is. At home, Rufus' parents are doing everything they can. They share books with him and encourage him to practise his early writing skills.

1. Identify how Rufus' development is linked to biological, genetic and inherited characteristics.
2. Identify the possible environmental influences on Rufus' development.
3. Explain how nature and nurture are both important in Rufus' development.

2.2 Biological and environmental factors

Five things to know ...

1. Development can be affected by biological factors.
2. Inherited characteristics and health conditions are examples of biological factors.
3. Development can also be affected by environmental factors.
4. Where children live and how their needs are met are examples of environmental factors.
5. It is likely that both biological and environmental factors will affect a child's development.

We have seen that development can be affected by nature or nurture or, in other words, by biological or environmental factors. In this section, we will look at some examples of these.

Biological factors

The genes that we are born with play a big part in our development. We have seen that genes and chromosomes can affect children's lives. These can cause health problems and may even affect how long a child lives. While these changes in genes are sometimes passed on from the biological parents, this is not always the case.

Inherited or health conditions

There are many ways in which we can see genes at work. Children often resemble their biological family in some way. They may also inherit some health problems.

- Muscle structure:
  Some children develop serious health problems because of their genes. An example of this is a disease called Duchenne muscular dystrophy. Over time, children's muscles weaken and this disease can cause an early death.
- Hair and eye colour:
  The type and colour of a child's hair and the colour of their eyes are also linked to the genes of the child's biological family. Genes might also affect how well children can see. Children who have parents who are short-sighted are also likely to become short-sighted.

Environmental factors

Environmental factors are the things that a child experiences that can affect their development. There are many different factors, so we will split them into different areas:

- location
- socio-economic situation
- family and lifestyle
- opportunities for exercise
- stimulation
- relationships.

Location

Where you grow up can make a difference to your development. Here are two examples of how location might affect a child's development.

Rural

- A child in the countryside may have more chance to play outdoors and learn about nature. This may help their physical development and health.
- For a child in the countryside, it may not be easy to visit places such as sports centres or cinemas.

Inner city

- A child in a city may have more opportunities to go to organised activities such as swimming or music lessons. This might help their social and cognitive skills.
- A child in a city may develop asthma because pollution levels are higher. They may have less space to play in.

Socio-economic situation

Research shows that how much money a family has can make a difference to development. There are many reasons for this. Parents or carers living in poverty may find it harder to afford the ingredients needed to cook healthy meals and this may affect children's health and development. Living in poverty, in other words being poor, can also affect parents' mental health. We know that if parents are stressed because of money worries, this can cause anxiety and depression. Depression can make it harder for parents to respond to their children or have the energy to play with them.

The amount of money a family has also makes a difference to housing. If a family does not have much money, they may not have much space. They may not have a garden or somewhere outdoors where it is safe to play. Poorer families might sometimes live in noisier places or in unsafe homes. This can affect children's health and their opportunities to play.

> **Activity**
>
> Think about where you grew up. What type of activities and opportunities were there?

Family and lifestyle

How well parents meet their children's needs can make a difference to development. Here are some examples:

Abuse

Some parents abuse their children or do not prevent others from abusing them. This can cause a range of problems. (See Unit 5 for more information on abuse.)

Neglect

Neglect is the term used when parents or carers are unable to look after their children properly. Parents may not know how to keep their children healthy, or they may not be able to do so because of an addiction. As a result of neglect, children may not have their basic needs met. Children may develop infections as a result of not eating properly or not having their hygiene needs met.

Drug/alcohol abuse

When parents are taking drugs or drinking too much, they are likely to abuse or neglect their children. Alcohol and other drugs may also cause mood swings in parents, which can be confusing or frightening for children.

Diet

What children eat and drink can affect their health and development. A healthy diet will help children to grow well and have enough energy. A poor diet may stop children from growing properly. Parents who have more money often find it easier to provide healthy food for their children.

> **Extend**
>
> Find out more about the likely effects on children's health if they are overweight or underweight at these websites:
>
> www.nhs.uk/live-well/healthy-weight/childrens-weight/overweight-children-2-5
>
> www.who.int/news-room/fact-sheets/detail/malnutrition
>
> Using the information on these websites, write down three ways in which adults can help young children be a healthy weight.

Opportunities for exercise

Children need to move in order to be healthy and also to develop physically. Most exercise for children under five happens when they play, especially outdoors.

Exercise is good for the heart and lungs. It is also good for developing healthy bones. During exercise, children develop physical skills such as learning to throw or kick.

> **Activity**
>
> Visit this website:
>
> www.nhs.uk/live-well/exercise/physical-activity-guidelines-children-under-five-years
>
> How much exercise should children under five be getting every day?

Stimulation

The brains of babies and young children develop quickly, but to do so they need stimulation such as playing with toys or seeing new things. Children who have stimulation have better cognitive development.

There are many ways to stimulate the brain. Here are two important examples:

- Language-rich environment:
  Listening and talking is sometimes called interaction. When there is a lot of interaction and activities such as sharing books or singing rhymes, we use the term 'language-rich environment'. When children are in a language-rich environment, their cognitive and language development is stimulated.
- Play experiences:
  When children have a range of play experiences, indoors and outdoors, all aspects of their development can be stimulated. This happens especially when adults talk to them during their play.

Relationships

Positive relationships with adults and children can make a difference to development.

With adults

The most important relationships in early life are those with parents and main carers. They can boost their child's confidence and help them learn how to be with others.

Relationships with other adults, such as teachers and nursery staff, will also affect children's development.

With other children

Some children grow up with other children in the family such as brothers or sisters. Other children may be the only child in a family.

Where relationships between children in a family are positive, there are benefits. These children should learn how to take turns, share and negotiate. Children will also learn these skills when they go to nursery or school.

> **Check what you know**
>
> Give an example of how a positive relationship with an adult can help a child's development.

2 Factors that influence the child's development

2.3 Effects of biological and environmental factors

> **Five things to know ...**
> 1. Biological and environmental factors can affect development positively as well as negatively.
> 2. Some effects are short term.
> 3. Some effects are long term.
> 4. Limited concentration is an example of a short-term negative biological effect.
> 5. Successful educational achievement is an example of a long-term environmental effect.

We saw that many factors affect children as they grow up. In this section, we look at the long- and short-term effects of these factors.

Biological factors

The effects of biological factors can be for the short term or long term. This depends on the biological factor and how much support the family and the child receives.

Short-term effects

Table 2.1 Short-term effects of biological factors on development

Short-term effects	How does this affect the child?	Example
Limited learning opportunities	Some health conditions affect whether children can do things that are useful for learning, such as listening or moving.	A child who has a chest infection may not be able to join in with physical activities.
Limited concentration when at a childcare setting	Some health conditions affect concentration. This might be because a child is feeling poorly or tired.	A child who is not sleeping at night because of eczema might find it hard to concentrate in nursery.
Withdrawn social behaviour/inhibited relationships with others	Children may not be able to spend time with other children or adults. This can affect their social development.	A child who picks up infections easily as a result of a medical condition may not have spent much time with other children.

Jargon buster

Eczema: a skin condition causing the skin to be dry and itchy.

Short-term effects	How does this affect the child?	Example
Insecure parental attachment	Parents may find it hard to bond with a baby or child who has a health condition or who is born early.	Bonding with a baby who cries a lot because of a health condition might be difficult, until the baby's health improves.
Secure parental attachment	Secure attachment can be affected in the short term.	A mother's post natal depression affects her ability to bond with her baby. After having treatment, she is able to form a secure attachment.

Exam-style question

1. Identify two short-term effects of biological factors on a child.

Long-term effects

Where a biological factor is ongoing or the child does not receive sufficient support, there might be long-term effects on their growth and development.

Reduced educational attainment

Some children may not achieve at school because of a biological factor. A child might often be absent because of illness or receiving treatment. Some children may also have a learning difficulty caused by a biological factor, such as Down's syndrome.

Limited range of career choices

Children's career options are often linked to how well they do at school. This can be difficult for children affected by biological factors.

Declining growth

Some inherited and genetic conditions are known as **degenerative**. Children slowly lose co-ordination and muscle tone. An example of this type of condition is Duchenne muscular dystrophy.

Mental illness

There are many ways in which children and adults can have mental illness. They include depression, eating disorders as well as substance misuse. Some children might develop mental illness if they are not coping with a health condition. In some cases, it is thought that certain types of mental illness, such as bipolar disorder, are genetic.

Mental illness can affect a child's social and emotional development. It may also affect a child's physical development, for instance if it is linked to an eating disorder.

Jargon buster

Degenerative: health conditions that reduce how much a child can do or learn over time.

2 Factors that influence the child's development

Difficulty in managing feelings

Some health and medical conditions affect children's emotional development. They may become frustrated if they cannot do what other children are doing. In some cases, a learning disability might make it hard for a child to use language to express their feelings.

Age-related milestones

Whether children achieve age-related milestones will depend on the biological factor. A child who wears glasses is likely to meet age-related milestones, but a child who has a significant learning difficulty might not. Whether children meet age-related milestones is also linked to how much support and how many opportunities they have.

> **Theory into practice**
>
> Rayan has Fragile X syndrome. It is an inherited condition. He has a significant learning disability and communication difficulties. He finds it hard to concentrate and is easily distracted. He also finds it hard to communicate with other children.
> 1. Identify two long-term effects on Rayan's development.
> 2. Biological factors can have long-term effects. How can these effects be reduced by receiving support?

Environmental factors

These can have a wide range of effects on children's development.

Short-term effects

Weight gain

Weight gain is linked to whether parents are giving their children the right amount of healthy food. Where a child is being neglected, they may not be given enough food. Where children are living in poverty, parents may not be able to pay for a wide range of healthy food.

Weight gain can be positive, but also negative. Children who have the right amount of healthy food will put on weight during their childhood. This is positive. Too little weight can mean that a child will not have sufficient energy for their physical development.

If children put on too much weight, this can cause health problems and make it harder for them to play and run around.

Positive feelings of wellbeing

Where families can meet children's needs, children are more likely to feel confident and also be healthy. Their **wellbeing** can be affected in the short term if the family's circumstances change, for example, divorce or illness.

> **Jargon buster**
>
> **Wellbeing:** how healthy and happy a person feels.

> **Jargon buster**
>
> **Deficiency:** a lack of one or more nutrients which may cause problems with growth and development.

Illnesses and deficiencies

Children have physical needs, and they require healthy food and clean air. If these needs are not met, children are more likely to become ill.

Where children are not eating a healthy diet, they may not take in enough nutrients. Nutrients, such as vitamins and minerals, are important for growth and health. The term for a lack of nutrients is **deficiency**. Some deficiencies have short-term effects. A deficiency of iron (a mineral) in their diet means that children will not have much energy. Once children start eating foods with more iron, they are likely to improve.

Age-related milestones

Where children's needs are being met, they are more likely to meet the age-related milestones. On the other hand, if children's needs are not being met for any reason, they are less likely to develop at the same speed as other children of their age.

Parental attachment

The child's relationship with parents can affect their development. Where children and parents have a strong or secure attachment, children's emotional and social needs will be met. Where parent attachment is weak or insecure, children are negatively affected and may show low levels of social and emotional development. Insecure parental attachment can happen when parents are depressed, stressed or are taking alcohol or drugs.

Long-term effects

Successful educational achievement

Children whose needs are met throughout their childhood are more likely to achieve at school and college. This will give them more career choices. They may also feel good about themselves.

Limited range of career choices

Where children's needs are not met, they are more likely to have fewer career choices because they may not have the confidence or the qualifications that are needed.

Thriving growth and healthy body weight

Children who have a healthy diet and who are not anxious are more likely to have a healthy body weight. This will help their physical development, and also their emotional and social development.

Nutritional deficiency

Some deficiencies caused by a lack of one or more nutrients cause long-term problems. A good example of this is vitamin D and calcium. They are both needed for the strength of bones and teeth. A lack of vitamin D and calcium can cause problems with teeth and bones later in life.

2 Factors that influence the child's development

Pain
Childhood trauma caused by abuse, neglect or poor diet can cause long-term health conditions, some of which may cause pain.

Expected milestones
Expected or age-related milestones are likely to be reached when children's needs are met over the long term. Where children's needs are not met over a period of time, they are likely to show delay in one or more areas of development.

Positive emotional wellbeing
Children whose needs are met over a long time are likely to have confidence. They will be able to express their feelings and develop relationships with others. This will give them positive **emotional wellbeing**.

> **Jargon buster**
>
> **Emotional wellbeing:** positive emotional state.
>
> **Transition:** the change from one stage, place or person to another.

Activity
Make a list of long-term effects that might be caused by both biological and environmental factors.

2.4 Transitions

Five things to know ...
1. Transitions are changes in children's lives or to their routines.
2. Transitions can affect children's development.
3. Some transitions can be planned for, i.e. expected.
4. Some transitions are sudden, i.e. unexpected.
5. Transitions can affect children's development in positive as well as negative ways.

During a child's life there will be many changes, often known as **transitions**. Examples of these transitions are:

- starting nursery
- going to a childminder
- moving school
- having a new sibling.

Some transitions will be important and have long-term effects on a child's growth and development.

Transitions may be positive for a child, such as moving to a larger home. Others may be negative, such as not being able to see friends.

> **Activity**
>
> Make a list of transitions or changes to your circumstances that you had between the age of three and five years.
>
> Compare these to someone else in your group. Are there any transitions that you have in common?

> **Exam-style question**
>
> 2 What does the term 'transition' describe?
>   a Opportunities children have at home
>   b Types of childcare that are available for families
>   c Approaches to working with children
>   d Changes that take place in children's lives

2.4.1 Types of transition

> **Five things to know ...**
>
> 1 Transitions can be expected or unexpected.
> 2 Transitions that are expected can be planned for.
> 3 Transitions that are unexpected are often sudden.
> 4 Starting at a school or childcare setting is an example of an expected transition.
> 5 A death of a family member or friend is an example of an unexpected transition.

Transitions can be put into two groups: expected and unexpected.

Expected transitions

Expected transitions can be planned for, and adults may be able to help children to prepare. Figure 2.2 shows some examples of expected transitions.

2 Factors that influence the child's development

Figure 2.2 Types of expected transition

Check what you know

Give two examples of expected transitions.

Unexpected transitions

An unexpected transition is one that is not planned. It may be quite sudden.

Table 2.2 Unexpected transitions

Type of unexpected transition	Examples
Bereavement due to losing someone or something that is important to a child	■ Sudden death of a friend, family member or pet
Change to family circumstance/dynamic	■ Reduction to household income ■ Eviction because rent is not paid
Family structure and separation	■ Parents may split up ■ A parent may have a new partner ■ A family member may move in

Exam-style question

3 Explain what is meant by the term 'expected transition'.

Check what you know

Give an example of an unexpected transition.

35

2.4.2 The impact of transitions on the child's development

Five things to know …

1 Transitions can affect children's development.
2 Transitions can affect development in positive or negative ways.
3 Each area of development can be affected by transitions.
4 Learning new fine motor skills would be an example of a positive effect.
5 Finding it hard to concentrate would be an example of a negative effect.

Jargon buster

Regression: when a child's development goes back to an earlier stage.

Chronic illness: a long-term health problem.

Self-care skills: skills that make children independent, such as dressing, feeding and toileting.

Transitions can sometimes be positive. They can give children more opportunities or help them to develop stronger relationships.

Other transitions can be negative and cause children to feel anxious. When children are anxious, their development can be affected in a number of ways. In this section we look at how transitions can have negative as well as positive effects on children's development.

Physical effects

Table 2.3 Negative and positive physical effects of transitions on children

Negative effects from transition	Explanation
Loss of or increased appetite	Children might not feel hungry, or they might cope by eating more.
Sleeping patterns, nightmares	Children might find it harder to sleep well and might have nightmares.
Wetting/bedwetting	Toileting accidents or bedwetting can happen when children are anxious.
Regression	Some children may 'go back' in their development, e.g. suck fingers or have toileting accidents.
Ill health	When children are feeling anxious, they are more likely to catch colds and other illnesses.
Chronic illness	Chronic or long-term health problems such as asthma might begin or become worse.
Positive effects from transition	**Explanation**
New fine and gross motor skills	Some transitions give children more opportunities to play and learn skills, e.g. starting at a pre-school.
Independence with self-care routines	A new setting or adult carer might encourage a child to master **self-care skills** such as dressing or feeding.
Access to new healthy food choices	A new setting or a family getting more money might mean that children eat a healthier diet.

2 Factors that influence the child's development

Cognitive effects

Cognitive development is about how children learn, take in information and think.

Negative impact of transitions

Young children might find change difficult because they cannot understand what is happening and why. This can cause them to become stressed and upset.

When children are stressed, they might find it hard to concentrate or remember things.

Stress can also affect healthy brain development as children might not feel like exploring or trying things out.

Positive impact of transitions

When a transition is positive, children might have new experiences which will help them learn, such as looking at books or singing counting songs.

Children might also develop some new skills to deal with challenges. They may, for example, learn to tidy their things so as not to lose them.

When children have lots of new opportunities to learn, this can help their brain to develop.

Communication and language

During and after a transition, some children may find it hard to express their needs and feelings. This can be a result of stress.

It can also happen when children are cared for by a new adult. Some children who can talk well may regress. When children have difficulty with talking and expressing their feelings, this can cause a delay in their speech and language.

On the other hand, a transition can be positive for a child. They might be with adults who help them to talk more. They might go to a new place where they can play with other children, and there might be more opportunities to talk.

Social and emotional development

Transitions can have a serious impact on children's social and emotional development. Children are likely to experience a range of strong emotions. Figure 2.3 gives some examples.

> **Check what you know**
>
> Give an example of why a transition might be positive for a child's cognitive development.

NCFE CACHE Level 1/2 Technical Award in Child Development and Care

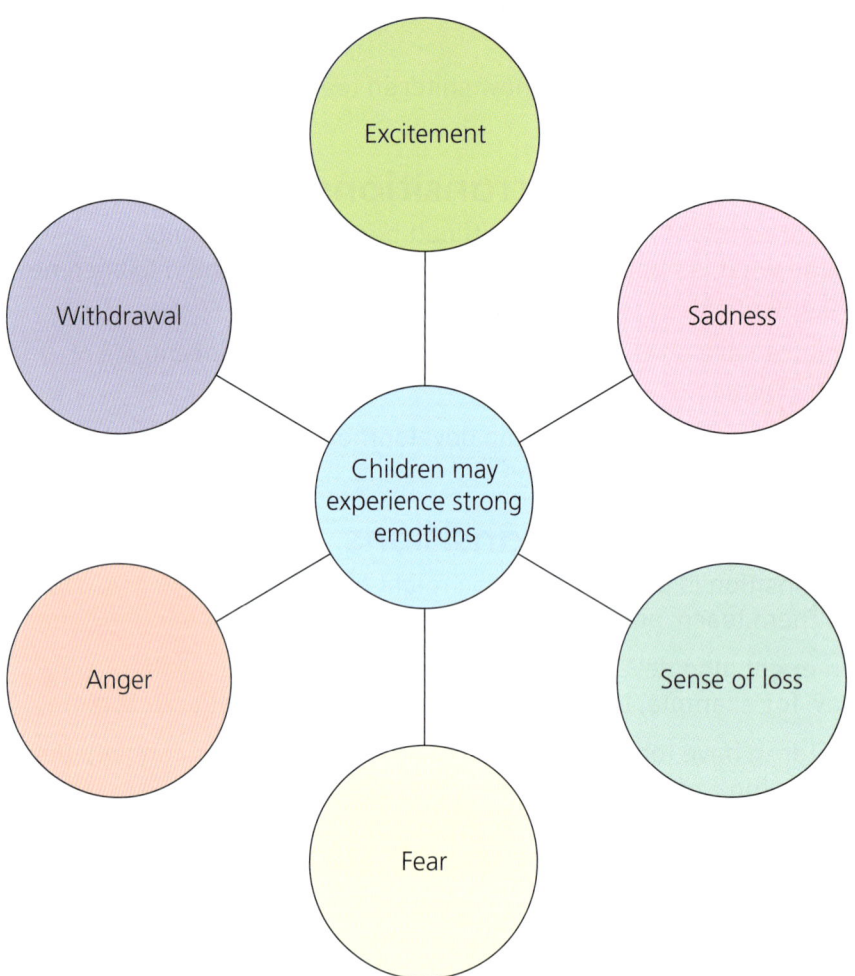

Figure 2.3 Strong emotions caused by transitions

Check what you know

Look again at Figure 2.3.

How many strong emotions can you write down from memory?

Check what you know

The term 'regression' was used earlier in this unit. Write down what this means.

Jargon buster

Resilience: the ability to cope with setbacks and problems.

Recognising children's emotions

Children may show their emotions in different ways, including:

- crying
- biting
- kicking
- becoming clingy
- regression.

Children's emotional wellbeing

Children's emotional wellbeing can also be affected.

- Some children cope well with the challenge and bounce back from any difficulties. This is known as **resilience**.
- Other children develop anxiety, depression or show unwanted behaviours such as biting.

2 Factors that influence the child's development

Experience interaction with new role models
Transitions can be a chance to meet new adults and children. This can be positive as children learn from watching them and interacting with them.

Gain confidence to manage and cope with new feelings
Transitions can be positive for children. They might learn that they are able to cope with change and strong feelings.

> **Activity**
>
> Draw four squares. Write one of the following areas of development in each square:
> - Physical
> - Cognitive
> - Communication and language
> - Social and emotional.
>
> In each square, write three possible negative effects of a transition.

> **Exam-style question**
>
> 4 Give **one** example of a negative effect and **one** example of a positive effect on a child's physical development as a result of a transition.

2.5 Support strategies

> **Five things to know ...**
>
> 1 Adults can support children with transitions.
> 2 Early years practitioners need to build a positive relationship with the child and their family.
> 3 Children need to have opportunities to express and talk about their feelings.
> 4 Professional help is sometimes needed to support children with some transitions.
> 5 Early years practitioners use specific strategies to help children with some types of transitions.

Adults can help children to cope with transitions. This can reduce the negative impact on their development.

NCFE CACHE Level 1/2 Technical Award in Child Development and Care

> **Jargon buster**
>
> **Child-centred approach:** when adults focus on what children need and want.

Key principles

We will start by looking at three key principles of supporting children:

1. Build positive relationships with the child and family.
2. Adopt a **child-centred approach**.
3. Provide experiences for expression.

Build positive relationships with the child and family

If relationships are good with the child and their family, information can be exchanged. This is important as everyone needs to know what is happening and what the child knows.

Practitioners also need to make sure that children's care needs are being met, as this is important for the child and the family. Table 2.4 lists some points to remember when building positive relationships with the child and family.

Table 2.4 How to build positive relationships

How?	Why?
Share information and use effective communication	■ To make sure that everyone has the information that they need ■ To make sure that information is prompt and clear
Show respect	■ To help communication and build relationships
Set clear boundaries	■ To make sure that the relationship stays professional
Be sensitive to needs	■ To recognise that parents and children may have particular needs
Establish care routines	■ To make sure that children's care needs are met in line with parents' wishes

Adopt a child-centred approach

It is important to focus on children's needs and how they may be feeling. This is known as a child-centred approach.

To do this, adults have to get to know children well, and understand their needs and interests. This is valuable when planning activities to help them with transitions. Adults have to be realistic with children when doing this: a child in a family where the parents have separated might want their absent parent or carer to return home, but this might not be realistic.

Children also need adults to be consistent in meeting their care needs. This might include having a clear routine for meals, washing and naps. A consistent approach can help children feel more secure.

Provide experiences for expression

Adults need to help children express their emotions and also talk about their fears and feelings. Activities and experiences can be planned to help with this.

> **Check what you know**
>
> What are the three key ways in which children can be supported before and during a transition?
>
> For each way, give a practical example.

Examples of activities that can be planned are:

- Imaginative play (see also section 3.2.2, page 57): this might include dressing up, and playing with play people or toy animals.
- Sensory experiences: this might include playing with water, sand or dough.
- Sharing books with the child: this might include books about the type of transition, such as going to nursery or saying goodbye to a friend.

Specific ways to support expected transitions

When a transition is expected, adults can prepare children over time. Here are some common transitions and examples of how to help children.

Starting a new childcare or education setting

Going to a new school or childcare setting can feel like a big step for children. Adults need to help them know what to expect and help children gain a sense of belonging.

- Visits: visiting the setting before starting is a good idea because children will see where they will be going. They might also meet the people who will be looking after them.
- Key person visits the child at home: the key person can see children in a familiar environment and get to know them. They can also find out more about what the child enjoys doing.
- Read books about starting school/setting: this can help children to ask questions or talk about how they are feeling.
- Use role play to play 'schools': this can help children prepare for school life.

Birth of a new baby

The birth of a new baby can change things in a family. Children will cope better if they have been prepared for the change.

- Play with dolls and toy prams: this can help a child to feel 'grown up' as they now have their own baby to care for.
- Read books about the birth of a new baby: books can help adults give information and also help children to know what to expect. Children may also have questions.
- Visit a family where they have a new baby: seeing a new baby can help children learn about babies' needs. They can also hear how babies sound when they cry and what parents do to care for the baby.
- Help choose toys or clothes for the new baby: this can help a child feel more involved. They might feel grown up because they are making some decisions.

> **Read and write**
>
> Create a simple book that will help prepare a child for the birth of a new baby.

Planned hospital admission

Going into a hospital can be scary. Children cope better when they know what to expect. Here are some ways of helping children:

- Visit the hospital prior to admission: this can help children see where they will be going.
- Watch a children's TV programme or film clip about a hospital: this can help children learn more about what people in hospitals do.
- Use doctors' or nurses' costumes for dressing up and play: pretending to be a doctor or a nurse can help children to feel more in control. Adults can also use this as a way of providing information about what will happen, such as lying down to be examined.
- Look at the hospital website to see pictures of staff and facilities: this can help children see who might be involved in their care. They can also see what a children's ward looks like.

Specific ways to support unexpected transitions

Bereavement of a friend or family member

Children will find it hard to cope with a death of a friend or family member. It can be a long process but children can be helped if they understand what is going to happen. They also need to have opportunities to talk about the person who is dying or has died.

Jargon buster

Bereavement: when a close family member or friend dies.

- Read books about **bereavement**: books where an animal or a human dies can help children talk about their feelings. It can also be a way to help children understand what is going to happen or what has happened.
- Create a memory box with special objects and photographs: a memory box can help children talk about their memories and feelings. Creating a box helps children to feel that they have some control over what is happening.
- Sensitively talk about the person who has died: children will sometimes want to talk about the person who has died. They might just make a comment, or they might want a long conversation. It is important that adults are sensitive about what they say.

2 Factors that influence the child's development

> **Extend**
>
> Find out more about how to support a child during or after bereavement. Look at this website and read through their information section:
>
> www.winstonswish.org

Change to family circumstance/dynamic

A family's circumstances might change for a number of reasons, such as unemployment or moving house. The dynamics or relationships in a family can also change when new people come to live with them or a person leaves. Children may need help in adjusting to these changes.

- Give an opportunity for discussion: it is important to listen to children and answer any questions when they raise the subject. You might need to stop what you are doing to show that you are available to talk to them.
- Together create a family tree: some children find it easier to understand what is happening when they see a family tree. A cousin might come to live with them, but they may not understand how this child or adult is related to them.
- Read books about different families: sharing books with children can help them make sense of what is happening to them. It can give them opportunities to ask questions.

> **Exam-style questions**
>
> 5 Flynn is three years old. He goes to nursery every day. His family members have moved in with his grandparents because they could no longer afford the rent on their own home. The grandparents' home is small and Flynn is now sharing a bed with his brother. Flynn's father does not get on well with Flynn's grandfather, and there are often arguments. Many of Flynn's toys have been put away as there is not enough space in the flat.
>
>   a Explain why it is important that the nursery has a good relationship with Flynn's parents.
>
>   b Explain two strategies that could be used to support Flynn with this transition.

NCFE CACHE Level 1/2 Technical Award in Child Development and Care

Family structure and separation/attachment issues

There are many reasons why a family structure may change. This may affect the relationship a child has with their parent. Divorce or the arrival of a new partner and their children are examples of this. There are various ways to help children with these issues.

- Access help from professionals: some families need support from other professionals. Schools and early years settings will often help families find this support.
- Read books about the situation: books can help children understand what is happening in their family. Children may ask questions or express feelings or comments while a book is being read to them.
- Spend time together as a family: it can be helpful for families to spend time together in order to build relationships. Settings can help families by providing suggestions of activities or games that they can enjoy together.

Test your knowledge

1. Explain the 'nature/nurture' debate.
2. Give one example of a biological factor affecting children's development.
3. Give three examples of environmental factors affecting children's development.
4. Give **two** ways in which **one** biological factor might have a long-term effect on a child.
5. Why might a child's educational achievement be affected by environmental factors?
6. What is meant by the term 'transition' in childcare?
7. Give an example of one unexpected transition and one expected transition.
8. Explain ways in which a transition may negatively affect a child's overall development.
9. Explain why it is important to support children before and during transitions.
10. Explain two ways in which an early years practitioner might help a child when they begin to attend a childcare setting.

Assignment practice

Case study
Lucy is four years old. She is at nursery, but will start at a local school soon. She has a learning difficulty caused by a chromosomal disorder. Her learning difficulty makes it harder for her to take in information. Her family is anxious about how well she will settle.

Task
Create a plan to help Lucy's transition. The plan should include:

1. An outline of the factors that need to be considered when drawing up your plan.
2. An explanation of three strategies that might be used to help Lucy's transition to school.

3 Care routines, play and activities to support the child

About this content area

When you work with young children, you will need to know about different care routines, play and activities so that you can support their independence, health, safety and wellbeing. By supporting their basic needs and planning play activities which promote their development, you will be enabling them to reach their full potential. In this unit, you will learn about basic care routines, and how to plan and support different types of play and activities.

3.1 Basic care needs
3.2 Basic care routines and play activities to support the child's development
   3.2.1 Basic care routines
   3.2.2 Play activities
3.3 The role of the early years practitioner during play activities

3.1 Basic care needs

Five things to know ...

1. Every child is unique, but their basic needs are the same.
2. These basic needs must be met so that children can grow, develop and reach their potential.
3. Children's basic needs are physical, emotional and **psychological**.
4. If children's basic needs are not met, this will affect their ability to develop, concentrate and learn.
5. Adults need to be able to support children's basic needs.

Jargon buster

Psychological: a condition which relates to the mind.

Hierarchy: placing items of a list in the order of importance.

Children rely on adults. They need adults to care for them and meet their basic needs until they are able to do this for themselves. However, being able to meet these needs depends on having certain conditions in place.

Maslow's hierarchy of needs

In 1943, a psychologist called Abraham Maslow developed his theory called a **hierarchy** of needs. He showed these human needs in the shape of a pyramid, starting from the most basic and moving upwards towards achieving our full potential. Maslow believed that certain conditions were needed for a human to develop. They could not move to the next stage until that need had been met. This is what he meant by a hierarchy of needs.

NCFE CACHE Level 1/2 Technical Award in Child Development and Care

```
           Self-
        actualisation
        
          Esteem
          
       Love and belonging
       
         Safety needs
         
       Physiological needs
```
Reaching full potential →
Basic needs

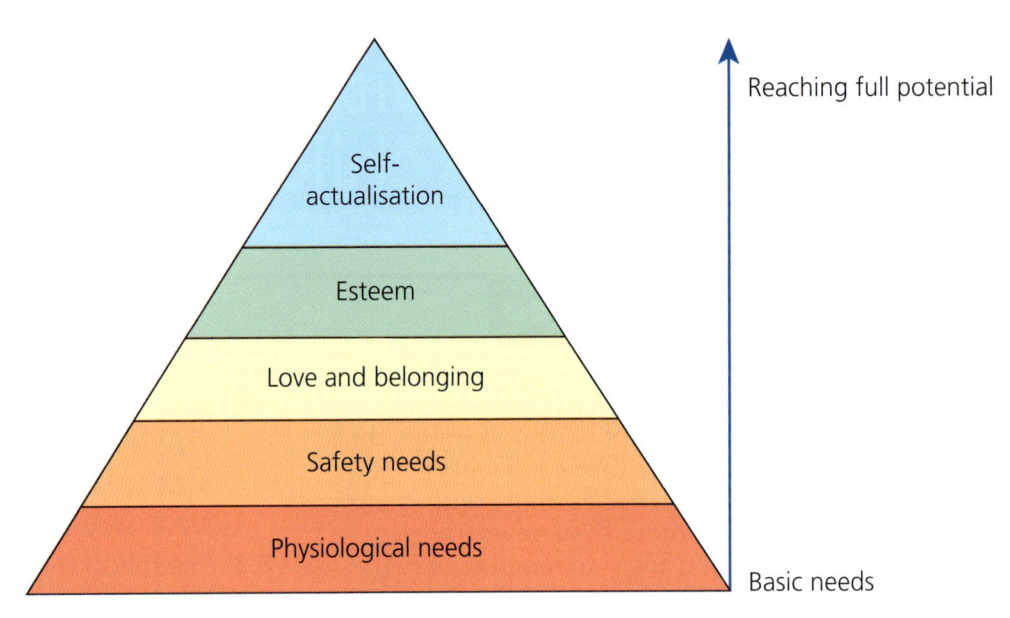

Figure 3.1 Maslow's hierarchy of needs

> **Jargon buster**
>
> **Physiological:** the way in which living things work or function.

Physiological needs

At the base of the pyramid are the child's **physiological** needs. These are what everyone needs in order to survive: air, water, nourishment, sleep, health, clothes and shelter. They are so important that they will always be the first basic human needs which should be met.

> **Read and write**
>
> What physiological needs have you met today? Think about basics such as washing, eating or getting dressed. How many can you list?
>
> Describe how you have learnt to do these things.

Safety needs

The next need is safety. If a child does not feel safe and is anxious or threatened, they will not be able to concentrate or focus on what is around them.

Routines and predictability help children to feel safe. This includes:

- emotional safety
- health and wellbeing
- freedom from physical fear.

> **Activity**
>
> What makes us feel safe? Make a list, ranging from the emotional reassurance of having family and friends to support you, to physical elements such as seatbelts in the car and a lock on a gate.

3 Care routines, play and activities to support the child

Love/belonging needs

Love and belonging are important to our emotional development. This means feeling part of a group and having unconditional love from parents and close family or friends.

There is an essential human need for relationships and feeling connected to others. This develops our own ability to feel that we belong and to give and receive affection.

> **Activity**
>
> Think about and list the different groups you belong to. These may include family groups, friends, those who share your hobbies, and people you have shared experiences with, such as classmates. How important are these groups for your own wellbeing?

Figure 3.2 Why is it important to meet children's love and belonging needs?

Esteem needs

Maslow divided esteem needs into two categories:

1. The need for self-esteem, through being independent and having a sense of achievement.
2. The need for respect from others, such as having a good reputation or status. In children, this is linked to the development of confidence and motivation in what they do.

Self-actualisation needs

This means being able to fulfil your **potential**. According to Maslow, this cannot happen unless all of the other stages on the pyramid have been met.

> **Jargon buster**
>
> **Potential:** what you are capable of.

> **Check what you know**
>
> Can you list the five areas in Maslow's hierarchy of needs? Put them in the right order, starting at the base.

> **Activity**
>
> Think about what you need to do before settling down to read a book or to study.
> - What do you need to have with you?
> - How important is it to be at the right temperature?
> - What happens if you are hungry or thirsty, or are feeling unwell?
>
> Write down your needs in order of importance. How well can you concentrate on what you are doing if your basic needs are not met?

> **Extend**
>
> Research Maslow's hierarchy of needs. Can you find out more about each area of need and why it is important?

Knowing about Maslow's model helps us to understand the importance of being able to meet children's basic care needs. These can be divided into two aspects:

1. basic needs
2. psychological needs.

Basic needs

Basic needs include those which Maslow classified at the lower end of the pyramid, such as physiological and safety needs.

Table 3.1 How to meet children's basic needs

Children's basic needs	Examples of how they can be met by adults
Food and drink	■ Providing healthy snacks and explaining why they are healthy ■ Providing access to drinking water at all times

3 Care routines, play and activities to support the child

Children's basic needs	Examples of how they can be met by adults
Fresh air	■ Planning regular opportunities for outdoor play ■ Providing trips to interesting places outside the setting
Rest and sleep	■ Making quiet activities available for children ■ Scheduling appropriate nap times
Exercise	■ Providing access to climbing and play equipment such as tricycles, trampolines or climbing frames ■ Offering times for physical movement such as dancing, and providing music or additional equipment
Physical safety	■ Checking equipment for faults ■ Making sure doors and gates are locked to secure the setting ■ Not using physical punishment
Emotional safety	■ Providing a consistent **key person** ■ Establishing key person interaction ■ Arranging small group play ■ Being a caring practitioner by looking after children's emotional needs ■ Ensuring bullying is not tolerated
Shelter	■ Providing a warm and welcoming environment ■ Providing areas shaded from the sun and sheltered from rain and snow

Early years practitioners should regularly think about how the basic needs of children and babies are being met and whether any changes can be made to improve provision for them. Meeting each of these basic needs should be part of the day-to-day organisation of the early years setting.

Jargon buster

Key person: a named member of early years staff who works with a specific group of children and their families.

Activity

Looking closely at Table 3.1, create a series of flashcards with the basic need on the front and ways in which it can be met on the back. Work with a partner to test one another.

Check what you know

Give three examples of ways in which early years practitioners can meet children's basic exercise needs.

Theory into practice

Michaela works in an early years setting. One of her responsibilities is to carry out a health and safety check each morning before the setting opens, which involves filling in a form to show that she has checked the outdoor area, equipment and furniture. She also has to check safety equipment such as stair gates, fire blankets and extinguishers.

1 Why is it important that this check takes place each day before the children come in?
2 How else can practitioners ensure that the environment is kept safe and secure for children?

Psychological needs

Psychological needs are more abstract than basic needs. This means that they relate to our thoughts and feelings.

These needs are found towards the top of Maslow's pyramid. They include having a sense of belonging, showing affection and developing a sense of achievement. Children's psychological needs must be met so that they can:

- grow in confidence
- develop a sense of who they are and where they fit in.

Table 3.2 How to meet children's psychological needs

Psychological need	Examples of how it can be met by adults
A sense of belonging	- Responding to the child's interests by being enthusiastic about what they say - Encouraging the child to join in with an activity or game - Providing opportunities to interact with others
Affection	- Comforting a child when distressed - Showing **empathy** by telling children that we understand how they feel
A sense of achievement	- Praising the child's efforts - Recognising positive behaviour
A sense of being valued	- Displaying the child's artwork - Showing an interest in the child's culture, for example by asking about religious or cultural festivals - Listening attentively to the child and giving eye contact - Recognising the child's needs
Establishing emotional boundaries	- Providing consistency with rules - Helping children to understand why rules are important

Jargon buster

Empathy: being able to understand another person's feelings.

Check what you know

How can early years workers support young children's sense of belonging?

Figure 3.3 How does a display of their work help young children to feel valued?

3 Care routines, play and activities to support the child

Exam-style question

1. Rioletta is three years old and is new to your setting. You are her key person; you know that she is a refugee and that the nursery environment is her first time away from her family. She speaks English as an additional language, as do her parents, and there are many gaps in their understanding.

   Rioletta has been clingy with her mum and unsettled during her first few weeks at nursery. She is not interested in taking part in activities with other children, preferring to play on her own. You know that the family are waiting to be housed and that they have moved several times since arriving in the UK three months ago.

   You and other staff are concerned about Rioletta and have asked her parents to come into the setting for a meeting along with a translator to talk about how best to support her.

   Using what you know about children's basic and psychological needs, describe why Rioletta may be finding it difficult to settle into the setting.

3.2 Basic care routines and play activities to support the child's development

3.2.1 Basic care routines

Five things to know ...

1. Routines support children's independence as they learn to practise these skills regularly.
2. Routines develop a feeling of predictability, which is important for the development of the child's confidence as they learn what happens next.
3. Routines enable adults and children to talk through what is happening, which supports language development.
4. Routines promote children's health, safety and wellbeing.
5. Routines support the development of good habits from an early age.

Table 3.3 shows some of the ways in which basic care routines support and promote a child's development.

51

Table 3.3 How care routines promote development

Care routine	How it promotes development
Getting dressed/changed	■ Choice in what to wear and what to do first ■ Chances for decision making – when is it time to get dressed or changed? ■ Building self-esteem by developing independence ■ Practising fine motor skills when fastening clothes
Mealtimes	■ Chances for decision making, e.g. what to eat ■ Self-reliance, e.g. feeding themselves ■ Problem solving – how many children will be sitting here? ■ Discussing the need for a healthy diet and what foods to eat ■ Developing fine motor skills
Toileting/washing routine	■ Self-care and independence ■ Self-reliance and knowing what to do next, e.g. washing hands before eating ■ Fine motor skills – being able to manage clothing ■ Protection from infection by knowing about hand washing
Rest and sleep	■ Healthy wellbeing, and knowing when and why rest is needed ■ Choice and knowing when they need to nap as they get older ■ Decision making in knowing when to get up ■ Self-care and being able to meet their own needs

Getting dressed/changed

Getting dressed is a good opportunity to support different areas of development. Adults can:

- talk it through with children and help them to decide when it is time to get dressed or undressed
- encourage children to work out what clothes they will need, and what needs to happen next as they get dressed.

As children become older and more independent, this routine also supports the development of their fine motor skills as they learn to attach poppers and fasten buttons, coats and shoes.

Mealtimes

As well as being a good opportunity to develop relationships with children, mealtimes are also a chance for adults to talk to them and develop their speaking and listening skills. They may also discuss the importance of a healthy diet for the child's growth and development, or apply problem-solving skills, such as 'How many cups do you think we need?'

Learning to feed themselves is an aspect of children's self-reliance as they become more independent and make decisions about what they would like to eat, or whether they have finished their food.

3 Care routines, play and activities to support the child

Mealtimes are also an opportunity for children to develop their fine motor skills, for example when using a spoon or fork.

Figure 3.4 Can you identify three ways in which mealtimes develop children's independence?

> ## Exam-style question
>
> 2 Describe how getting dressed supports the development of each of the following:
>   a decision making
>   b fine motor skills
>   c self-esteem.

Toileting and washing routines

While babies and toddlers need adults to change nappies for them, routines are still required for this, and for older children's toileting in the setting. Washing hands after using the toilet and changing nappies should be part of the routine, as well as before handling food or eating and drinking.

For children, these routines will also develop their skills of self-care and self-reliance. Adults can talk to them about the importance of hygiene and protection from infection.

Rest and sleep

Rest and sleep are very important to young children's health and wellbeing. They need to have periods of quiet and sleep during the day. The setting should have routines in place for babies and young children so that they can have quiet periods away from play activities. There will be gradually less need for this as children grow and develop.

If they feel tired, older children should be able to choose when they can go for a nap. This also supports decision making and learning about self-care.

> **Check what you know**
>
> Give two examples of care routines which will promote the independence and health of the child.

> **Extend**
>
> Find out about the amount of rest and sleep young children typically need during the day at the following ages:
> - six months
> - one year
> - two years
> - three years.

3.2.2 Play activities

When thinking about play activities, it is important for us to remember that play is one of the ways in which children learn. Play can be planned or unplanned, and can be initiated by adults or children. Play also supports children's holistic development and can involve different types of activities and resources.

> **Five things to know …**
>
> 1. Play activities are a key part of the way children learn.
> 2. They are holistic and can include all areas of a child's development.
> 3. Children can take part in play activities independently or in a group.
> 4. Play activities can be supported by adults.
> 5. Play activities can be planned or unplanned.

Physical play

Physical play encourages …
- Balance and co-ordination
- Control of fine movements
- New concepts
- Confidence
- Healthy wellbeing

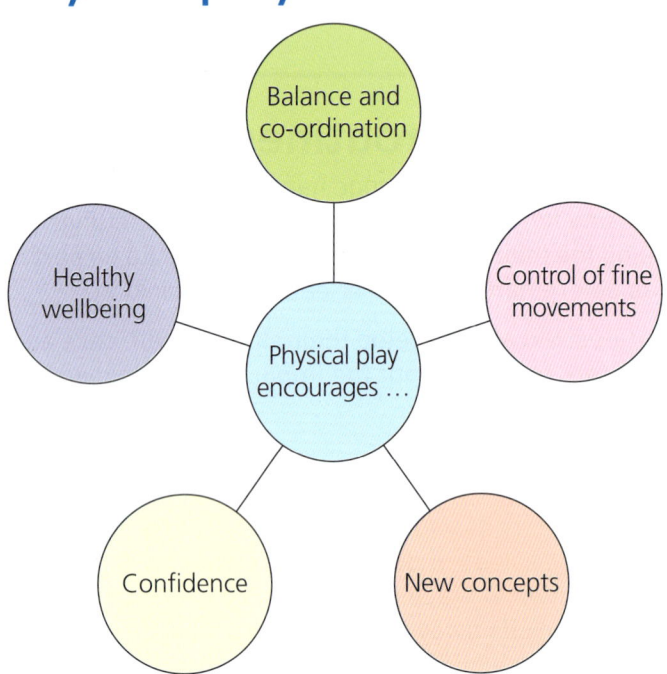

Figure 3.5 Physical play involves a range of fine and gross motor skills to support different aspects of a child's development

3 Care routines, play and activities to support the child

Most play activities which children take part in have some kind of physical aspect to them, as the first stages of learning are linked to their practical, physical experiences. Physical play involves the child's fine and gross motor skills, and develops different areas:

Balance and co-ordination

These gross motor movements involve the child's arms and legs, and are developed by activities such as throwing and catching a ball, hopping and skipping, running and jumping, climbing on apparatus and riding on pedal toys or scooters. These activities develop muscle strength and support co-ordination.

Control of fine movements

Activities which support the development of fine motor movements might include rattles, clay and dough, mark making and drawing, threading beads, smaller construction toys and using a spoon or fork. Practice in carrying out these types of activities will allow children to develop greater control of their fine movements.

New concepts

Physical play supports children in the development of new concepts and ideas, and in making sense of the world around them. It allows them to explore their environment safely, both alongside their peers and with adults.

Confidence

Developing physical skills helps young children to develop their confidence and self-esteem. They will start to understand the potential risks involved when carrying out activities such as climbing and running, and learn to think about how to plan their physical movements carefully.

Healthy wellbeing

Physical play is an important part of children's wellbeing. Outdoor play in particular develops physical exercise, which is important for a healthy heart and muscle strength. It also develops children's social and emotional skills as they learn to take turns and think about one another's needs.

Exam-style questions

3 Ralf is working in a nursery. As part of his role, he regularly takes children outside where they have access to a range of play activities and equipment.
  a Identify three resources which Ralf might put outside to develop children's physical skills.
  b Describe the other areas which might be developed when carrying out these activities.

Check what you know

What is the difference between fine and gross motor skills? Give an example of one of each.

NCFE CACHE Level 1/2 Technical Award in Child Development and Care

Jargon buster

Media: the way in which types of art are expressed, for example through paint, drawing or music.

Child-centred: putting the needs of the child first and encouraging them to be independent.

Creative play

Creative play allows children to explore and experiment with different **media**, such as junk modelling, paint, chalk, clay or musical instruments, and natural resources such as twigs, pebbles and mud. It is important that children are provided with plenty of different resources which encourage them to explore and develop their own ideas.

Although practitioners may be tempted to 'help' children with creative activities to make them look or sound more appealing, it is important to remember that the activity itself rather than the end product is part of the learning process, and should be as **child-centred** as possible.

New language

Through creative play, adults can introduce children to new language and vocabulary, for example when talking about different types of music or painting, and when discussing how to develop their ideas. Adults can talk to children as they are carrying out activities and comment on what they are doing to reinforce their language and introduce new vocabulary.

New concepts

Creative play gives children opportunities to explore new concepts which they may not have experienced before, often through the use of natural resources or junk modelling. It also gives children opportunities to explore their environment and use their imagination.

Confidence

Children's confidence is developed through creative play as they are able to explore their own ideas through different media. Staff in early years settings will also create displays to show others, which will support children's self-esteem.

Problem solving

Creative play gives children opportunities to solve problems as they work out how to develop their ideas. For example, they may have been given resources for junk modelling and have to make decisions about how they are going to build a car or a house. Adults can also support them in doing this through the use of effective questioning as well as talking about what they are doing and why.

Theory into practice

Sandy is working with Brian and Vikram, who are both four. They are outside and have been playing with some natural resources. They want to build a den using sticks, leaves and branches so that they can hide inside it. They have started by leaning some larger sticks against a tree which has fallen over.

1 How is this play activity supporting Brian and Vikram's learning?
2 How could Sandy support them without helping them to build the den?

Check what you know

Name two ways in which creative activities help children to develop their confidence.

3 Care routines, play and activities to support the child

Imaginative play

Imaginative play allows children to explore and experiment using different scenarios in a safe environment. Children can use their imagination to:

- make sense of the world around them
- develop relationships with their peers
- refine their communication and physical skills.

For imaginative play, children can use small world figures and dolls, puppets, dressing up clothes and role play areas.

Expression of feelings

Through imaginative play, children learn to think about their own feelings as well as those of others, as they imagine themselves in different situations. For example, in a role play area they could be in a shop and need to think about what to say and do in their character's situation, depending on whether they are buying or selling.

Control of fine motor skills

Children will use these skills as they manipulate and control the different resources, for example using a puppet or fastening dressing-up clothes. They will also use these skills in the role play area if they need to write, such as filling in a form or writing a prescription in a doctors' surgery.

Relationships and communication

Imaginative play supports the development of these skills as it encourages children to co-operate with one another. They need to be able to express their needs as well as listen to the thoughts and ideas of others.

> **Check what you know**
>
> Give two examples of how imaginative play can be used in early years settings.

Sensory play

Sensory play is an opportunity for children to use and stimulate their senses and learn through exploration. This means that they will be able to smell, see, feel or hear something different from their usual everyday experiences.

For sensory play, children could use different types of dough (for instance, **scented dough**), slime, cornflour, sand, water, shaving foam, paint or musical instruments. Natural materials, such as mud, sticks and water, should also be involved throughout children's outdoor learning experiences. They should be given a range of these experiences on a regular basis to explore how these things feel, smell and sound. This will also benefit their learning and development in various ways.

> **Jargon buster**
>
> **Scented dough:** a type of playdough with an added smell or scent, such as lavender.

Expressing feelings

Children can use these materials to express sensory reactions. For example, they may just wish to rub their hands in shaving foam or paint, or feel and squeeze slime as it runs through their fingers. They might use paint or dough, or explore a mud kitchen, to create shapes or designs which show how they are feeling. As children's language develops, adults can talk to them about how the different materials make them feel and about the smells, sounds and textures which they are experiencing.

Hand–eye co-ordination

Through sensory play, children develop their hand–eye co-ordination as they look at and explore a range of resources. They use their hands to squeeze and manipulate materials, and learn how their actions affect what is happening.

New concepts

Sensory play encourages children to develop new concepts as they work with different materials. They might add water to dry sand and talk about the difference between the two, or find out about different ways of mixing materials together. Sensory play encourages children to think independently as they have control over what they are doing.

Concentration

Sensory play can encourage young children to concentrate for long periods of time as they become more involved in what they are doing and develop their ideas. This helps to develop connections in the brain which enable them to have more complex thoughts.

Activity

Play a game of 'recall tennis' with a partner:
- Take it in turns to name different types of play activities.
- You can have one point for each correct answer but remove a point if you get any wrong.

Exam-style question

4. Which one of the following is a type of sensory play?
   a. Playing with dough
   b. Threading cotton reels or large beads
   c. Small world play
   d. Cutting and sticking

Read and write

Create a flyer for a new nursery to show some of the different play activities which will be on offer, and how they will support children's learning and development.

Jargon buster

Early Years Foundation Stage (EYFS): this sets out the requirements for children's learning and development from birth to five years.

Exam-style question

5. Your setting is planning a topic on animals for the three- and four-year-old children. The team are having a planning meeting and have asked everyone to think about different activities for the topic.

   Create a heading for each of the seven **Early Years Foundation Stage (EYFS)** areas of learning, and suggest two activities for this topic beneath each heading.

3 Care routines, play and activities to support the child

There is more about the EYFS, including the areas of learning, in Unit 4, section 4.2.

3.3 The role of the early years practitioner during play activities

According to the EYFS,

> 'Play is essential for children's development, building their confidence as they learn to explore, relate to others, set their own goals and solve problems. Children learn by leading their own play, and by taking part in play which is guided by adults.'
>
> (Statutory Framework for the EYFS, 2021)

Five things to know ...

1. Early years practitioners should be able to offer children a wide range of activities and opportunities.
2. The learning environment should be safe and well resourced.
3. Children's behaviour should be well managed.
4. Children's needs and interests should be met.
5. Early years practitioners should listen to children's ideas and promote their independence.

We have looked at ways in which play helps children to learn. We now need to think about how the early years practitioner's role influences children's play – before, during and after play activities.

Before learning activities

Complete a risk assessment or safety sweep

This means checking the learning environment for any hazards and thinking about the level of risk so that action can be taken if necessary.

All early years providers are required by law to make sure that their premises are safe, and the EYFS requirements state that the premises, environment and equipment must be fit for purpose. For example, if you find a broken piece of furniture, a child might hurt themselves on it so it should be removed from the learning environment straight away.

> **Extend**
>
> Using the most up-to-date version of the statutory framework for the EYFS, research the health and safety requirements in section 3. What do they say about keeping the environment safe?

Consider how to meet children's individual needs and interests

Early years practitioners need to get to know the children in the setting so that they can think about how to meet their individual needs and interests. This will usually be developed through the key person as they will have the closest relationship with their group of children.

The EYFS states that:

> 'Practitioners must consider the individual needs, interests and development of each child in their care, and must use this information to plan a challenging and enjoyable experience for each child.'

This means that if a child is interested in a particular topic, they should be given the opportunity to talk about it and explore it further in the setting. This could also be included as part of a topic area and the planned activities, and is likely to motivate the child to learn more. A wide range of appropriate equipment and resources should be planned to ensure that all children have equal opportunities to access different activities, including specialist equipment for those with specific needs.

> **Theory into practice**
>
> Ryan is working in an early years setting with Mohammad, who has a strong interest in trains. He brings one into the setting with him each day and can tell Ryan all about different trains he has seen and where he has seen them.
>
> Ryan would like to incorporate Mohammad's interest into some of the setting's planning.
>
> 1. Why is it important to think about Mohammad's interest in trains when planning learning activities?
> 2. Name two ways in which trains could be incorporated into the setting's plans.

Complete planning documentation

All early years settings have documentation which sets out **long-**, **medium-** and **short-term plans**. These plans help practitioners to provide a range of activities during the year and make sure that they are covering the different areas of the EYFS curriculum. Plans also include timings, staffing and necessary resources.

> **Jargon buster**
>
> **Long-term plans:** topic plans which are set out over a year.
>
> **Medium-term plans:** termly or half-termly plans.
>
> **Short-term plans:** plans for a week or a day.

3 Care routines, play and activities to support the child

Identify outcomes for children

When planning and carrying out learning activities, early years practitioners need to identify learning outcomes. This means that they should be clear on what they want children to be able to do by the end of the activity. This will help practitioners to work out whether the activity has been effective. For example, if children are pouring and filling using different containers in the water, the learning outcome could be for the children to use the language of 'more' and 'less'.

Theory into practice

Sam has set up a learning activity using coloured rice, red and blue counters and tweezers: the children will try to pick up the counters with the tweezers and sort them into a different container for each colour. Sam knows that this activity will support the children's fine motor skills and mathematical development, but has not put this into words as a learning outcome on his short-term plan.

1. Why is it important to be specific about learning outcomes?
2. What is the main learning outcome from this activity?

Prepare resources and the environment

Early years practitioners are responsible both for setting up the environment and for preparing resources. When setting up an indoor or outdoor learning environment, they will need to ensure that:

- the environment is safe
- the resources are suitable for the age and developmental stage of the children
- the resources support specific learning activities.

Check what you know

Name three things which learning practitioners need to do before setting up learning activities.

Extend

Using the internet, have a look at some examples of short-, medium- and long-term plans for early years settings. What do you notice about each of them? Discuss in small groups.

During learning activities

One of the most important ways in which adults can support children during learning activities is by talking to them and questioning them about what is happening. This is important for children's speech and language skills, and will also enable practitioners to understand more about their individual needs. There are different ways to achieve this.

Engage in open-ended talk and discussion

Adults should use **open-ended talk** so that children are encouraged to have a conversation. For example, the adult could say 'Tell me about your painting' or 'How could we make a bridge to cross the river?'

Jargon buster

Open-ended talk: questions and conversations which encourage the other person to answer fully, rather than just replying 'yes' or 'no'.

NCFE CACHE Level 1/2 Technical Award in Child Development and Care

This might encourage the child to tell them about what they are doing and to use descriptive language.

Provide praise and encouragement

Encouragement is important for young children: they might not have come across a particular type of activity before or know how to approach it. They might also need encouragement to continue with a task if they are finding it challenging. Praise should also be given regularly, particularly if children are trying hard at a task and even if they are unable to complete it; this will motivate them to continue.

Figure 3.6 How can early years practitioners support children during play activities?

Theory into practice

Dilan and AJ are both three years old and are in the outdoor area. They are playing a game together and are trying to throw bean bags into a hoop on the ground. You notice that Dilan has managed to get a few bean bags into the hoop, but AJ is finding it difficult and is getting upset.

1. What could you say to AJ?
2. Why is it important that she has some encouragement?

Jargon buster

Commentary: talking about what is happening as it takes place.

Scaffold learning: providing support for learning through breaking it into small steps.

Focus on interacting to support activity outcomes

Adults should also encourage children to talk about the intended outcomes during the play activity. As well as providing a **commentary** about their progress, interacting during the activity will help to develop children's vocabulary. Adults can also support children by questioning them and can **scaffold** their **learning** when it is needed.

3 Care routines, play and activities to support the child

> **Extend**
>
> Find out more about scaffolding learning in the early years and how to do it.
>
> You could use this website:
>
> https://cheqdin.com/scaffolding-early-years

Encourage socialisation and co-operation between children

Socialisation and co-operation are an important part of children's experiences in early years settings as they are learning how to behave around others. While some might have limited experience of this, others might have a very sociable home life and mix with others outside the setting.

Encouraging children to play together and share the experience also encourages socialisation and develops these skills. Early years practitioners should always encourage children to support each other and talk to them if there are disagreements so that they can understand one another's point of view.

Facilitate practitioners' or peers' support to encourage children to solve problems

Early years practitioners should look out for opportunities to **facilitate** children's learning when they are carrying out activities, while being careful not to interfere with what they are doing. This means being sensitive and waiting for cues from them where possible. An example of this might be waiting to be spoken to by the child during an activity before starting to ask questions about their learning (see example in 'Theory into practice' below). Practitioners should also encourage children to support one another during play and learning activities. This gives them positive experiences of working with others and shows them the importance of listening to others' ideas and encouraging them to solve problems.

> **Jargon buster**
>
> **Facilitate:** organising the play environment to encourage learning.

> **Theory into practice**
>
> Anita is three years old, and your team has noticed that she regularly plays on her own. Although she seems happy doing this, you have been thinking about finding opportunities to support her socialisation skills.
>
> You notice that today she is playing on her own with some larger construction blocks. When you go over to her, she tells you that it is going to be a ship. She is trying to move a block which is too heavy and you notice that another child, Nico, is standing close by and watching her.
>
> 1 What should you do in this situation?
> 2 How might this help Anita?

Listen to children's ideas

It is always important to listen to children, whether this is during play activities or during other times of day. They should feel listened to and know that adults take the time to talk to them about their ideas. This will support their self-esteem and help practitioners to understand their motivation for playing in a particular way.

> **Activity**
>
> Think about a time when you did not feel listened to, particularly if you felt you had something important to say. How did this make you feel?

The early years practitioner is responsible for ensuring that children are kept safe and secure at all times; this also applies when they are carrying out play activities. Children can become very focused on what they are doing and might not be aware of any dangers which occur as part of the activity, or in the environment around them.

Promote independence

Early years practitioners should always promote children's independence as much as possible. If a child asks for help, they should be given the tools for managing it themselves when this is possible, rather than being told what to do.

> **Activity**
>
> Think about a time when you have asked for help with something because someone older or more experienced is close by. Could you have tried to do it yourself? Why do you think this is important?

Manage children's behaviour

Young children sometimes get into arguments or disagreements when they are playing together. As well as being role models for behaviour, adults need to be able to talk through what has happened and encourage children to listen to each other's point of view or talk about how they may be feeling. This will support their ability to **empathise** with others as well as to **self-regulate** and think about the impact of their own words or actions.

Adapt the activity, interaction or resources to ensure inclusion of all

When working with young children you might find that not all of them are able to do all activities. This might be because:

- there is a problem with the resources
- the children have not understood what they need to do
- they have a specific physical or educational need.

Check what you know

Give three examples of potential hazards in an early years setting.

Jargon buster

Empathise: to see a situation from someone else's point of view.

Self-regulate: to be able to manage your own emotions.

3 Care routines, play and activities to support the child

If this happens, you might need to take time to talk it through with them, or to adapt the activity – change it slightly to ensure that they are able to do it. Adapting the activity could be through a physical change to allow for a child's needs or a change in the activity itself.

After learning activities

Tidy/clean up the environment and pack away resources

Early years practitioners are responsible for tidying up the environment and ensuring that learning resources and materials are put away safely in the right place. Children should be encouraged to join in as much as possible, as it is a good way of developing a sense of responsibility and learning to take care of their things.

The learning environment should be organised so that there are designated areas for different items, for example a book corner, or a cupboard for maths equipment. This will help everyone to find and put away resources easily.

Think about the effectiveness of the activity in meeting outcomes

All practitioners who work in early years should take time after play activities to think about how effective each activity was in meeting the intended outcomes. This means how much children were motivated by the activity itself and whether they enjoyed carrying it out.

Practitioners need to think about whether the activity was accessible to all children or whether it needed to be adapted while the children were carrying it out. Some activities take a long time to set up but are not a popular choice for children, and this may be a reason to approach them differently next time.

Reflect on outcomes achieved by children

Practitioners should always reflect on play activities after they have been carried out and think about what the children have achieved. In the case of child-led activities, practitioners should think about the level of the child's interest and engagement within the activity as well as the outcome.

> **Check what you know**
>
> Give four examples of the role of the early years practitioner during play activities.

> **Activity**
>
> Create a checklist which you could use at the end of the day to ensure that the environment has been tidied away effectively.

NCFE CACHE Level 1/2 Technical Award in Child Development and Care

Exam-style questions

6. Jenna has set up and carried out a play activity with groups of children to make tyre prints using paint and dough. Her learning outcome was for children to look at and compare the different tyre prints and to talk about them. She was then planning to display them afterwards to show the different patterns.

   However, as Jenna carries out the activity, she finds that the tyres do not print well as they are too small, and it is difficult for the children to compare them in any way.

   a Describe what Jenna should do at the end of the activity.
   b Explain why it is important for her to reflect on the activity.
   c Outline what she might do next time to change the activity.

Test your knowledge

1. Describe what is meant by children's 'basic needs'.
2. How does Maslow's hierarchy of needs influence how practitioners meet children's basic needs?
3. Explain the difference between basic needs and psychological needs.
4. Give **one** example of a care routine.
5. How do toileting and washing routines support children's development?
6. What type of play might include musical instruments?
7. How might sensory play encourage the development of new concepts?
8. Name **three** types of plans which may be used in early years settings.
9. Explain what we mean by 'open-ended talk'.
10. Why is it important to reflect on the effectiveness of play activities?

Assignment practice

Case study
You are working in a nursery with three- and four-year-old children. The next topic will be teddy bears, and the children will be reading the story 'Goldilocks and the Three Bears'.

Task
1. Think about some play activities which could be planned for the children, using the story as a starting point.
2. Produce a plan for this topic which includes:
   - headings for the areas of physical, creative, imaginative and sensory play
   - lists of play activities for each category
   - notes which identify how each activity might support children's learning and development.

4 Early years provision

About this content area

The term 'early years provision' refers to a wide range of places where babies and children receive childcare and education. In this unit, we look at the type of settings they might go to and why early years provision is important. We also consider different varieties within the same type of setting.

4.1 Types of early years provision
4.2 The purpose of early years provision
4.3 Types of early years setting
4.4 Variation in early years provision

4.1 Types of early years provision

Five things to know ...

1. Who pays for early years provision can vary.
2. Some early years provision is paid for by the government.
3. Some early years providers need to make a profit.
4. Some early years provision is provided by charities and not-for-profit organisations.
5. Children may go to more than one type of provision.

Early years provision and how it is paid for is very complicated. There are three main types of provision.

1. **Statutory** provision: this is required by law. A good example of a statutory provision is a primary school. The government has to provide and pay for schools.
2. Private sector provision: this is a privately owned setting, run as a business to make a profit. They do this by charging parents/carers or claiming fees from the government for sessions. Many nurseries used by working parents are privately run. These nurseries are often open all year round and for long hours.
3. **Voluntary provision**: this kind of setting is run to make a difference to children and their families. Their aim is not to make money. They may

Jargon buster

Statutory: something that is required by law.

Voluntary provision: not profit-making as the aim of the organisation is to support families.

67

NCFE CACHE Level 1/2 Technical Award in Child Development and Care

> **Check what you know**
>
> What are the three main types of provision?

be given money from government. A lot of voluntary sector early years provision is run by charities or not-for-profit organisations. They may work closely with local authorities to provide some services, such as out-of-school clubs.

Activity

Private businesses often have websites that end in '.com' or '.co.uk'. Voluntary early years settings often state on their websites that they are run by a charity or are not for profit.

- Type 'Find a nursery in x' into your web browser, adding in the name of your nearest town or city.
- Choose two websites from the results and see if you can work out what type of early years provision they are.

Exam-style question

1 Which of these is an example of statutory early years provision?
   a A community pre-school
   b A reception class in a school
   c A childminder
   d A nursery

4.2 The purpose of early years provision

Five things to know ...

1 Early years provision promotes all areas of children's development.
2 Early years provision allows parents/carers to work or undertake training.
3 Early years provision may give families a break.
4 Most early years provision follows the statutory framework for the EYFS.
5 Early years provision can help children develop the skills and knowledge set out in the EYFS.

There are three main reasons for early years provision:

1 To promote holistic development.
2 To support parents or carers.
3 To promote the prime and specific areas of learning within the statutory framework for EYFS.

4 Early years provision

Promoting holistic development

Children in early years provision are likely to play and do activities that help their overall development. They will also be with adults who are trained to support children's development. Here are some examples of how children's holistic development may be helped by early years provision.

Physical development

Children may have more space to run and play in. In early years provision, there may be resources that can help physical development, such as tricycles and climbing frames.

Cognitive development

In early years provision, children have opportunities to do new things, which will help their brain development. This is because new experiences, interesting resources and opportunities to talk to adults and other children can stimulate the brain. Children may develop new interests and have opportunities to develop their problem solving.

Social and emotional development

Early years provision can support children's social and emotional development. At the setting, children might:

- play with other children and make friends
- learn how to be with others as part of a group.

Language and communication

Children's language and communication skills may be developed. Through playing with other children and talking to adults, they can develop their verbal and non-verbal skills. Being in an interesting environment and having new experiences is likely to increase opportunities for communication.

Supporting parents or carers

When children attend early years provision, it can help parents or carers. Being with young children takes a lot of time and it is often hard for parents to do anything other than look after them. Here are some things which early years provision helps parents to do.

Seek or retain employment

Some parents/carers need their babies and children to go to an early years setting so that they can go back to work. They may need the money and may also have a career that they do not want to give up.

Some parents need their babies and children to attend early years provision because they need to look for work. They may be claiming benefits and are required to look for work. Universal Credit is the way most people receive benefit payments in the UK.

NCFE CACHE Level 1/2 Technical Award in Child Development and Care

> **Extend**
>
> Visit this webpage:
>
> www.gov.uk/government/publications/universal-credit-and-your-family-quick-guide/universal-credit-further-information-for-families.
>
> What are the rules if a lone parent has a child aged three years and is claiming Universal Credit?

Receive respite

Jargon buster

Respite: having a break from caring.

Respite care gives parents or carers some time off from looking after their children. There are many reasons why respite care may be needed. It may be that a child has significant medical needs or a disability. It may be that a parent or carer has their own health or other needs. Respite care lets parents or carers have a break while knowing that their child is benefiting from being in an early years setting.

Access training opportunities

Some parents or carers use the time that their children are in early years provision to:

- develop new skills
- start a training course
- attend higher or further education
- begin an apprenticeship.

Participate in recreation and leisure activities

Check what you know

Can you write down the three main reasons for early years provision?

Some parents/carers use the time when their child is in early years provision to do something of interest to them, such as swim, play a musical instrument or spend time with friends and family.

Promoting the prime and specific areas of learning within the statutory framework for EYFS

We have seen that early years provision can help children's overall development. To make sure that all settings are working in ways that help children make progress and keep them safe, the government introduced an early years framework.

Here are some key points about the EYFS:

- The EYFS covers provision for all children aged 0–5.
- Nearly all early years settings are required by law to follow this framework, including reception classes.

The framework is divided into two sections: safeguarding and welfare requirements, and learning and development requirements:

- The safeguarding and welfare requirements outline how the setting must work to keep children safe and secure.
- The learning and development requirements list the knowledge and skills that children will need to do well in school and to enable opportunities to fulfil their potential.

Areas of learning and development and the Early Learning Goals

Seven areas of learning and development are described within the learning and development requirements. They are divided into prime and specific areas.

The prime areas are seen as the building blocks for later development. They are:

- personal, social and emotional development
- communication and language development
- physical development.

To check that very young children are making progress with the prime areas, there is a progress check for two year olds if they attend early years settings.

The specific areas of learning and development are:

- literacy
- mathematics
- understanding the world
- expressive arts and design.

To check that children are making progress, each area of learning and development sets goals for children to achieve. These goals are called **Early Learning Goals**. Children's progress in meeting these goals is checked at the end of the reception year (Early Years Foundation Stage profile). The child's level of development must be assessed against the Early Learning Goals to determine whether they are meeting expected levels or emerging (not yet reaching expected levels).

Jargon buster

Early Learning Goals: targets for the skills and knowledge that children should have developed by the end of the reception year (Early Years Foundation Stage profile).

Check what you know

Can you remember the prime areas of learning and development in the EYFS?

> **Activity**
>
> Download a copy of the EYFS from:
>
> www.gov.uk/government/publications/early-years-foundation-stage-framework--2
>
> Find the learning and development requirements section.
>
> Can you write down one of the goals for communication and language?

> **Exam-style question**
>
> 2 Explain how early years provision might benefit parents.

4.3 Types of early years setting

> **Five things to know ...**
>
> 1 There are different types of early years setting.
> 2 Some settings look after babies as well as older children.
> 3 Some settings are open for long hours.
> 4 If parents/carers use a crèche, they have to stay on the premises.
> 5 Childminders are based in their own homes, so have the smallest settings.

Different types of setting

There is a wide range of early years settings. Here are some descriptions of different types.

Crèche

Crèches are different to other types of early years provision: parents can leave their children, but they must stay on the premises.

Crèches care for children until they are eight years old for short periods of time, such as two hours. Crèches can be provided in shopping and leisure centres. They might be set up for parents/carers to attend a short course or information session. Crèches can be used by parents regularly or just from time to time.

4 Early years provision

Childminder

Childminders work in their own homes to look after children of any age.

Childminders have to follow the EYFS for any child aged 0–5 years. There are rules on how many children they can care for at the same time. Parents might use childminders before and after school or for the school holidays. Childminders often work throughout the year.

Figure 4.1 A childminder works from home

Nursery

Nurseries, or day nurseries as they are often called, take children from as young as three to six months until five years. Some take older children before and after school, and also in the school holidays.

To help working parents, nurseries are usually open all year round and they have longer opening hours than most other types of setting, such as 7 a.m. to 6 p.m. Most nurseries offer morning, afternoon and all-day sessions.

Pre-school

Pre-schools are sometimes known as playgroups. They usually accept children from two years old until they start school.

Many pre-schools run in community spaces such as church halls or community centres. Most offer morning, afternoon or day sessions, but these are normally shorter than nursery sessions. Many pre-schools only open during the school term.

Nursery class

Nursery classes are usually led by early years teachers or teachers with qualified status working alongside early years practitioners. Many are part of a primary school. Nursery classes operate during term time. They usually take children aged three to four years old for morning or afternoon sessions. Sometimes children may attend a full day.

Primary school

Primary schools take children from four to eleven years. By law, children must attend from the term after their fifth birthday, but many children start primary school in the September of the school year that they turn five years old.

Primary schools open during term time. Most primary schools start around 9 a.m. and finish between 3 p.m. and 4 p.m.

To help working parents/carers, many schools provide before and after school care. Funding for before and after school places is usually linked to families' incomes and individual needs. Some schools also have holiday clubs. Before/after school care and holiday clubs are often run in partnership with others, such as charities.

Activity

Local councils and authorities are required to provide information for families about childcare in their area.
- Visit the website of your local council or authority. Input your postcode and make a list of childcare provision within one mile of your home or college.
- How many different types of early years setting are there?

Exam-style questions

3. A parent is looking for an early years setting for their six-month-old baby for 30 hours a week.
    a. Identify two types of early years setting that accept children of this age.
    b. Explain the difference between them.

4.4 Variation in early years provision

Five things to know ...

1. Not all early years settings are the same.
2. Parents/carers have to make decisions about what will work best for them and their child.
3. Cost, opening times and location are often important factors for parents.
4. Settings will offer different things, such as outdoor space or a wider range of resources.
5. Settings might have different approaches to how they work with young children.

4 Early years provision

We have seen that there are many different types of early years setting. We have also seen that, although most provision will follow the EYFS, the purpose of provision may vary. In this section we look at other ways in which early years settings may be different to each other.

Accessibility

Not every family will be able to send their child to some early years settings. Table 4.1 provides some reasons why people might not be able to access the setting.

Table 4.1 Factors that affect a setting's accessibility

Factor	Why does this make the setting inaccessible?
Cost	If settings are charging fees, the cost may be too high for some parents/carers.
Eligibility and admissions criteria	Some early years settings only take children in certain circumstances, such as: ■ parents must be receiving benefits ■ families must be living locally.
Location	Some early years settings are in places which are hard to reach by public transport, such as a Forest school based on a farm. Other early years settings might be easy for families to reach, or be convenient because they are close to a parent's place of work.
Opening times	Early years settings have different opening times. ■ Some have longer opening hours than others. ■ Some settings are only open during the school term, while others are open throughout the year.

> **Jargon buster**
>
> **Eligibility and admissions criteria:** the rules set down by an organisation about which children or families can attend the setting.

Capacity

The EYFS has requirements that all early years settings have to follow. They include requirements about:

- how many children a setting can accept
- how many staff or adults there should be.

Number of children

The number of children allowed in a setting depends on how much space a setting has, but also how many members of staff. The EYFS has different requirements for different types of early years setting:

- A reception class can have no more than 30 children, for example. Some schools may be large and so have two or more reception classes.
- This is different from childminders, who are allowed no more than three children aged under five.

Figure 4.2 The EYFS states how many adults are required to the number of children

> ### Extend
>
> Download a copy of the EYFS. Look at the safeguarding and welfare requirements section, and find the premises section.
> - What is the minimum space required for every two-year-old child?
> - Work out how much space a nursery would need to have in order to have 16 children aged two years.

Ratio of staff to children

The EYFS has requirements about how many adults are needed to care for different ages of children – the **ratio of staff to children**. The number of staff needed depends on:

- the age of the children
- the qualifications of the adults
- the type of setting.

A nursery or nursery class of three-year-old children and a qualified teacher has a maximum ratio of 1 adult to every 13 children. Without a qualified teacher, the same setting is allowed 1 adult for every 8 children.

While minimum ratios are set out in the EYFS, some settings choose to have many more adults working with children. This might mean that children get more attention or can do more interesting activities.

> **Jargon buster**
>
> **Ratio of staff to children:** the proportion of staff to the number of children.

> ### Extend
>
> A pre-school is looking at its staffing numbers for next term. It will have 14 children aged two years and 28 children between three and four years.
>
> Using the information in the statutory framework for the EYFS, calculate how many staff in addition to the manager will be needed.

Facilities

If you ever visit early years settings, you will see that they are all different. Some have large indoor spaces, while others have good outdoor spaces. Here are some examples of how **facilities** may differ.

Indoor environment

Some early years settings have a lot of space. Others may be smaller but feel cosier.

Many settings that accept children of different ages split them up by age groups, such as a baby room and a toddler room.

Some settings have a hall for dance, yoga or PE, while others have a library.

Outdoor environment

Some settings have large outdoor spaces, even including woods, vegetable patches and ponds. Others may have a very small space and so will take children to the local park.

The way that outdoor spaces are arranged can also vary:

- Some settings have large open areas.
- Other settings divide the spaces so that there are different areas of learning.

Resources

The equipment and toys can vary between settings:

- Some settings avoid having plastic toys and focus on having natural resources.
- Some settings have a good stock of books, while others have lots of opportunities for children to paint and make things.

The resources that settings use often link to children's stage of development as well as their interests. Some settings may also have specific resources that will support children with special needs or disabilities.

Approach

There is more than one way of working with children. We can see that different settings organise things differently because of their approach.

Learning activities

In some early years settings, children spend a lot of time choosing what they want to do and exploring resources. In other settings children spend more time doing **adult-led** activities. This is where adults tell them what to do and show them how to do things.

> **Jargon buster**
>
> **Facilities:** places or equipment that an early years setting can offer.
>
> **Adult-led:** activities or play that is organised and led by adults.

5 Legislation, policies and procedures in the early years

About this content area

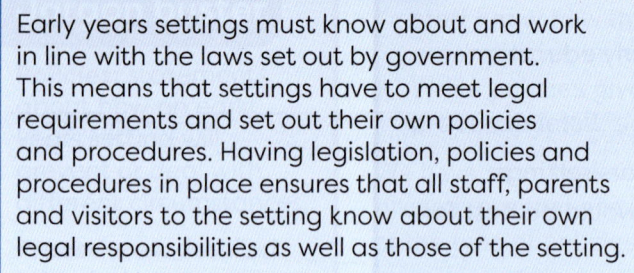

Early years settings must know about and work in line with the laws set out by government. This means that settings have to meet legal requirements and set out their own policies and procedures. Having legislation, policies and procedures in place ensures that all staff, parents and visitors to the setting know about their own legal responsibilities as well as those of the setting.

All early years practitioners need to be up to date and familiar with the key policies and procedures covered in this unit.

5.1 Regulatory authority
5.2 Legislation and frameworks which underpin policy and procedure
   5.2.1 Legislation, framework, policy and procedure definitions
   5.2.2 Legislation
   5.2.3 Health and safety procedure
   5.2.4 Equality and inclusion procedure
   5.2.5 Safeguarding procedure
   5.2.6 Confidentiality procedure

5.1 Regulatory authority

Jargon buster

Regulation: rules made by an authority to control the way something is done.

Standardisation: creating standards for all settings.

Five things to know ...

1. Most industries and public sectors have a regulatory authority to look over and enforce **regulations**.
2. The regulatory authority for early years and educational settings is called Ofsted.
3. Ofsted stands for Office for Standards in Education, Children's Services and Skills.
4. All registered early years settings are inspected by Ofsted at least once every six years.
5. Anyone can look at the Ofsted website, which shows the report of a setting's latest inspection.

A regulatory authority is a group which has been created by the government to manage different professions or organisations, such as financial services, health or education. The authority has a **standardisation** process, setting up certain standards and making sure that organisations keep to them.

5 Legislation, policies and procedures in the early years

Office for Standards in Education, Children's Services and Skills (Ofsted)

Ofsted is a government department which is non-ministerial. This means that it is not directly political and has no power to change legislation. It is known for carrying out inspection visits and writing reports on education settings. It also has other responsibilities, described in Table 5.1.

Table 5.1 Ofsted's responsibilities

Ofsted responsibility	What this means
Inspects childcare, adoption and fostering agencies	Ofsted inspects education settings such as maintained schools and academies, colleges of further education and some independent schools. It also inspects childcare, adoption and fostering agencies, and initial teacher training.
Regulates early years and children's social services	Regulation by Ofsted creates a set of rules for settings such as early years and children's services, so that their responsibilities are clear.
Ensures services are suitable for children and vulnerable young people	The inspection and regulation process ensures that children and young people are protected, including the most vulnerable.
Completes inspection visits and reports on care services	Ofsted inspections are regularly carried out on education settings and care services. Their findings are published and posted online. This helps policymakers, parents and the government to check the effectiveness of the settings and recognise their achievements. It also supports settings in looking at ways to improve.

5.2 Legislation and frameworks which underpin policy and procedure

Check what you know

List three of Ofsted's responsibilities.

Five things to know ...

1. Legislation governs the way in which early years settings operate.
2. Staff need to know about and understand laws which relate to early years and why they are important.
3. All early years settings have a number of policies and procedures based on legislation.
4. Key policies and procedures are about safeguarding, health and safety, equality and inclusion, and confidentiality.
5. The EYFS statutory framework is a legal document which must be used in all early years and childcare settings.

5.2.1 Legislation, framework, policy and procedure definitions

Five things to know ...

1. Legislation means a set of laws which are set by government.
2. Frameworks are a set of standards that must be met.
3. Policies are an agreed set of actions which have been adopted by an organisation.
4. Procedure means the way in which a setting carries out its policies.
5. All organisations have policies and procedures so that everyone knows how they will be run.

You will need to understand the meaning of each key word in Figure 5.1, as you will come across them regularly when you work in early years settings.

Legislation
A law or set of laws that have been passed by Parliament

Framework
A set of standards that must be met

Policy
An agreed set of actions which have been adopted by an organisation

Procedure
The way in which a setting carries out a policy

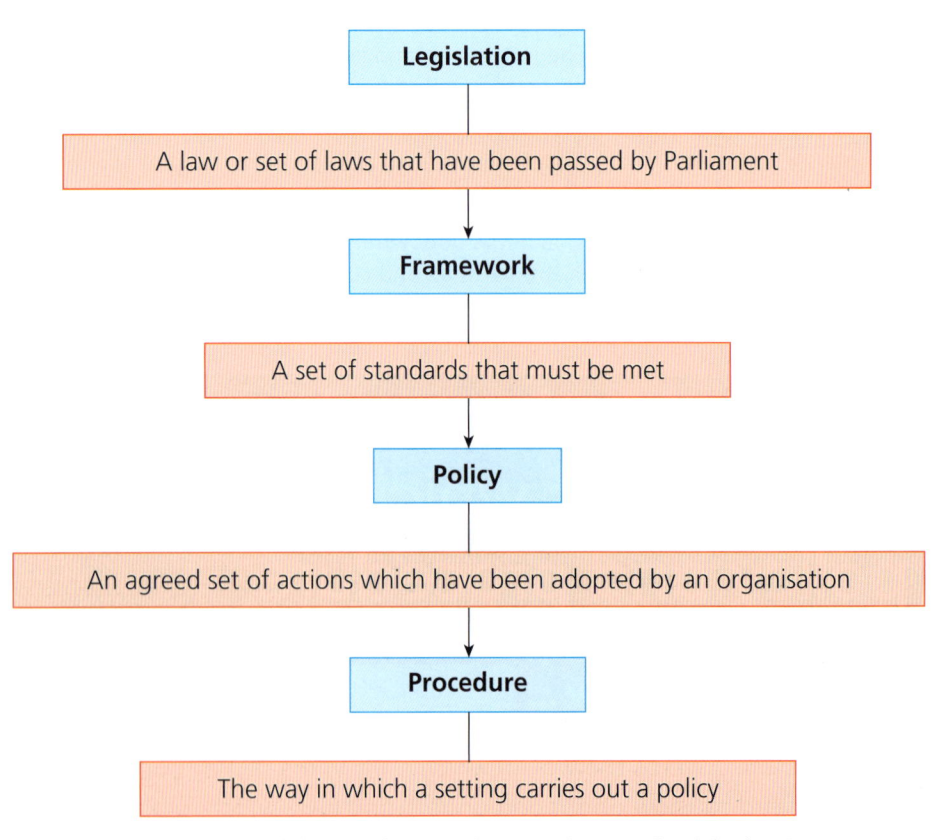

Figure 5.1 How do policies and procedures relate to legislation?

Activity

Put each of the main terms in Figure 5.1 into a sentence; for example, 'The setting had a policy of not allowing animals on the premises.'

5 Legislation, policies and procedures in the early years

5.2.2 Legislation

> **Five things to know ...**
>
> 1. Legislation is a process in the UK.
> 2. Legislation starts with a bill or law proposed by any Member of Parliament.
> 3. The bill is debated in Parliament; after the debate, the bill must be approved by each House of Parliament.
> 4. The bill receives Royal Assent.
> 5. The bill becomes law and is then called an Act.

There are a few key pieces of legislation which affect early years settings. These in turn influence policies and procedures, staff responsibilities and the way in which settings are run. All staff need to understand key legislation and policies so that they know what they need to do by law in the workplace. (For more detail on each procedure, see sections 5.2.3–5.2.6. For more on policies and procedures for attendance, behaviour and appearance, see Unit 6.)

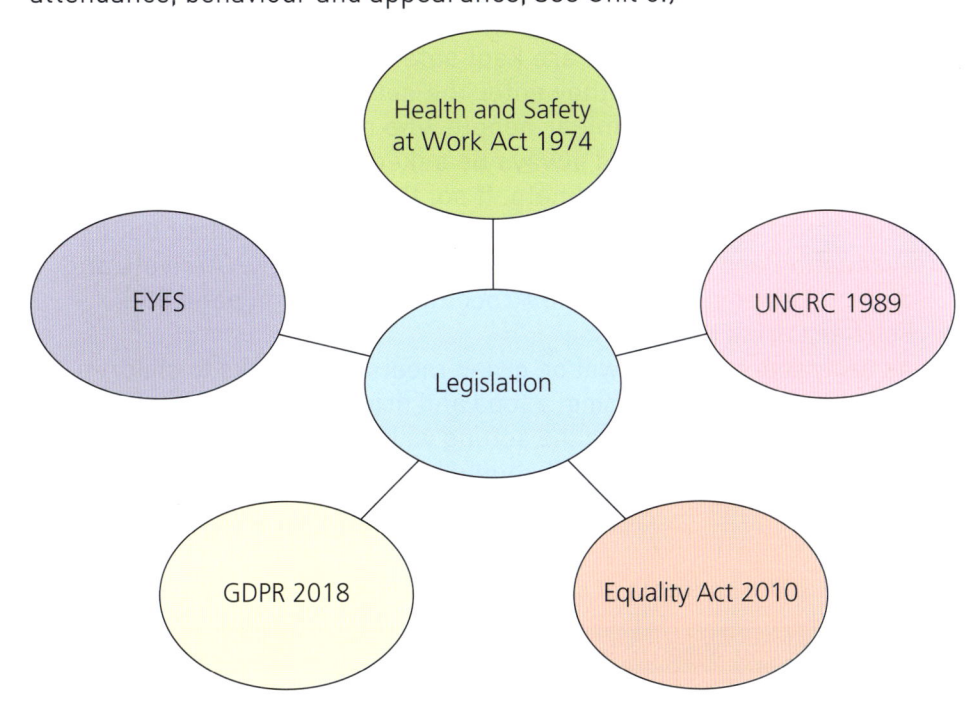

Figure 5.2 The important legislation for early years settings

Legislation:
- Health and Safety at Work Act 1974
- UNCRC 1989
- Equality Act 2010
- GDPR 2018
- EYFS

The Health and Safety at Work Act 1974

The Health and Safety at Work Act is legislation which affects workplace health and safety, and the welfare of children, staff and visitors within the workplace. This law:

- covers the maintenance and safety of buildings and equipment
- makes sure that working practices are safe.

Policy

All workplaces are required to have a health and safety policy under the Health and Safety at Work Act. In early years settings, it is important that children, staff and visitors are kept safe and well. The policy will set out the roles and responsibilities of both the setting and the staff, and include their agreed procedures for doing this.

The EYFS statutory guidance also gives information and guidelines about health and safety. (For more on the EYFS guidance, see page 91.)

Extend

Look online for the health and safety policy for an early years setting. Find out about four staff responsibilities under the policy.

Other policies in the setting will also relate to the Health and Safety at Work Act 1974.

- Visitors to the setting policy:
  The health and safety policy will include information about security and the importance of monitoring visitors to the setting so that children and staff are kept safe. Visitors should be signed in and given badges as they enter the setting so that they can be identified. Any unfamiliar people who are seen in the setting without visitor ID should always be asked if they know where they are going and if they need help. If so, they should be escorted to where they need to go. Visitors should also be told about building evacuation and safeguarding procedures. (See also 'Arrivals and departures of visitors' in the Procedure section on page 86.)
- Food and drink policy:
  As early years settings will be giving meals and snacks to children while they are at the setting, a food and drink policy is required. This sets out the ways in which the setting will ensure that food and drink are given to children safely. It should be read alongside the EYFS statutory guidance. Table 5.2 shows the guidance which needs to be included in the policy.

Table 5.2 The contents of the food and drink policy

Policy guidance	What this means
Guidance on food preparation	- Food will need to be stored and prepared safely, and staff should wash their hands before preparing and serving food. - Cultural differences and health requirements in food preparation and eating should be respected. - Staff should always be careful with equipment such as sharp knives, and ensure that they are washed and safely stored after use.

5 Legislation, policies and procedures in the early years

Policy guidance	What this means
Food and drinks to avoid	Some foods should be avoided at an early age. The government website has published a list of items to avoid for early years providers (see Extend activity below): ■ Before 6 months: cow's milk, eggs, foods containing wheat or gluten, nuts, seeds, fish and shellfish, honey. ■ Before 12 months: honey. ■ Up to 5 years: nuts, raw eggs, sugar, foods high in salt or saturated fat, unpasteurised milk/milk drinks and cheese, some types of fish and shellfish, raw jelly. Settings are also only likely to provide fresh tap water and plain milk. Water should be available for children at all times.
Supervision	It is important that young children are watched by adults when they are eating and drinking, and are not left on their own. Young children can choke on small pieces of food so there must be clear advice on the foods that can be given to them. Children should also be taught about: ■ basic food hygiene and the reasons for this ■ the importance of making healthy food choices.
Allergies	Settings must find out about any allergies or dietary/health requirements which children have so that they can plan and prepare foods appropriately. All staff will need to know about those children who have food allergies or intolerances.
Food hygiene	All food and drink will need to be prepared hygienically, and staff must have training in food hygiene if they are preparing and handling food for babies and children. Food hygiene is particularly important at this age as young children have immature immune systems, so will be more sensitive to food poisoning.
Preparing infant formula	Washing and sterilising bottles, teats and other equipment before each use is important, and the setting is likely to have a policy to follow when doing this.

Extend

Read the government guidance on food safety for children aged under five years:

https://help-for-early-years-providers.education.gov.uk/safeguarding-and-welfare/food-safety

Name three foods which should not be given to young children. What advice is given to reduce the risk of choking?

NCFE CACHE Level 1/2 Technical Award in Child Development and Care

Jargon buster

Equity: ensuring that each child has the resources they need to succeed.

- Equality and diversity or inclusion policy:
All settings require this policy, due to both the UNCRC and the Equality Act 2010. (For more on this Act, see below, and for procedure see section 5.2.4.) This policy is to ensure that every child is included in learning activities and that all children are given equal opportunities. Children should also be given **equity** in early years settings so that they are able to reach their potential.

Procedure

Procedures relating to the UNCRC will be detailed in the policies, but will cover the following points:

- Report abuse:
In all cases, early years settings must record and report any cases of abuse. The procedure should also outline what staff should do in cases of suspected abuse. (For more on safeguarding procedure, see section 5.2.5.)
- Provide play:
Procedures will set out how the setting provides a range of safe opportunities of indoor and outdoor play. They may also describe how practitioners should support children in a way which encourages their independence and creativity.
- Adapt activities:
All early years practitioners must be able to adapt activities where necessary to meet the needs of individual children and to help them make progress. This means providing additional equipment or resources so that the child is able to carry out the activity. For example, a visually impaired child might need additional time to touch and explore resources with their hands, or a magnifier so that they can look at a book clearly.

Exam-style questions

1. Reggie is three and a half years old and has a diagnosis of an autism spectrum condition. He has limited speech and dislikes changes to his routine. He loves dinosaurs and playing outside and wants to do this all this time.
    a. Outline the type of adaptations which the setting might need to make to support Reggie.
    b. Describe how practitioners can encourage Reggie to take part in a range of activities while supporting his needs.

The Equality Act 2010

The Equality Act was introduced to replace and update nine earlier equality laws in the UK. The law protects each person's individual characteristics and makes sure that everyone is treated equally.

There are nine protected characteristics under the Equality Act, which means that everyone in the UK is protected against discrimination for any one of these: see Figure 5.3. For example, pregnancy and maternity

5 Legislation, policies and procedures in the early years

are a protected characteristic, which means that it is illegal for someone to lose their job because they are pregnant or have a child. (For more on equality and inclusion, see section 5.2.4.)

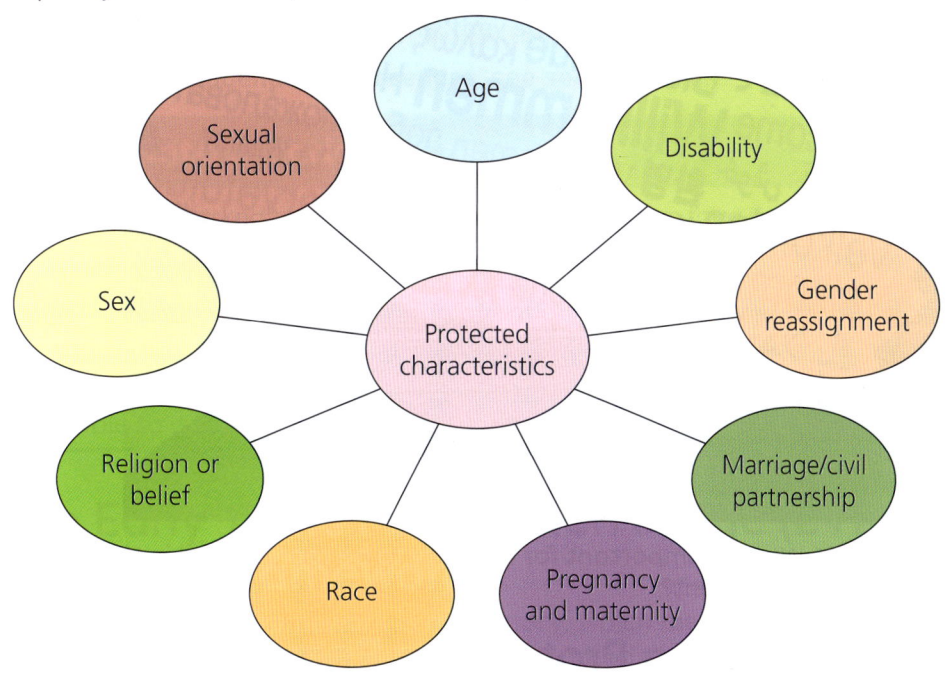

Figure 5.3 The characteristics protected by the Equality Act

Policy

The relevant early years policy to this legislation is the equality and diversity (or the equality, diversity and inclusion) policy. This will set out how the setting is **inclusive**, and values and supports children from all backgrounds and abilities, providing them with what they need to succeed.

Procedure

The setting will need to show that it is welcoming and inclusive to all. There are a number of ways in which it can do this. (For more on equality and inclusion procedure, see section 5.2.4.)

- Provide resources that reflect society:
  Early years settings should provide a range of diverse resources, such as toys and books, which positively reflect different groups within society. This is important to promote equity so that all children feel that the environment in the setting relates to them, and they start to recognise diversity in society.
- Be a good role model:
  Staff in the setting should be good role models as children copy adults and want to be like them. Being a good role model means showing children through your own behaviour how to behave and talk about others in a positive way.
- Adjust activities so that everyone can participate:
  Early years practitioners should make sure that they change activities where necessary so that all children are included. This might mean providing extra equipment or resources so that everyone can take part.

> **Jargon buster**
>
> **Inclusive:** something which is open to and includes everyone.

The health and safety policy should have information about:
- giving medicines and first aid to children
- how the premises are kept safe and secure
- how accidents are reported.

Procedure

The EYFS sets out various procedures which should be clear and easy to follow, and staff should be made aware of these.

- Ensure adequate staff–child ratio:
  The setting must follow the correct staff–child ratios and have the qualifications which are set out in the EYFS statutory guidance. This applies to all early years settings, including childminders.
- Respond to **disclosure**:
  This means that if staff are told anything which means that a child may be at risk, they must record and report this to the DSL. If a child tells them anything, they must respond sensitively. (For more on this, see section 5.2.5.)

Jargon buster

Disclosure: making information known to others.

Activity

The EYFS states that the guidance document 'What to do if you're worried a child is being abused: Advice for practitioners' is useful. It is on the gov.uk website.

Find a copy of this document online. What is the advice if a child tells you that they have been abused or neglected?

- Never use personal mobile phones when working with children:
  All staff, volunteers and anyone who is in the setting should be aware that they should never use their own mobile phones when working with children. This includes taking pictures of children, even if they are for the children's records. The setting will have its own equipment which should be used for this purpose, so that children are protected.

Theory into practice

You have no childcare qualifications and are just starting your childcare course. You are working with a childminder who regularly has more than three children under five in her care. You have asked her about this, but she has told you that as two of them are her own children, and you are with her, this is fine.

1. Should you tell anyone about your concerns?
2. Why is it important that the correct ratios are used in all early years settings?

5 Legislation, policies and procedures in the early years

5.2.3 Health and safety procedure

> **Five things to know ...**
>
> 1 Health and safety procedures mean making sure that all children and adults in the setting, in the outside area and on visits are kept safe.
> 2 Health and safety is the responsibility of all staff; everyone must remain vigilant.
> 3 There will be a health and safety representative in the setting so that staff can report any concerns.
> 4 Equipment and the environment will need to be regularly checked.
> 5 Risk assessments need to be carried out when planning a new activity as well as for general day-to-day routines such as food safety and maintaining security.

All staff in early years settings are responsible for maintaining health and safety procedures on a day-to-day basis. This includes:

- checking the environment often
- removing and reporting anything which is not safe for children or other adults
- putting plans in place so that staff and children know what to do in hazardous situations.

All early years settings should also have a 'responsible person' who is required to ensure the safety of staff and children. This person is usually the employer or the owner of the building.

Your setting's health and safety policy will include its health and safety procedures.

Carry out risk assessments

Early years practitioners are asked to carry out regular risk assessments for:

- planning new activities
- taking children out of the setting
- setting security, cooking and food safety
- nappy changing
- fire safety
- one-off events such as bringing an animal into the setting.

The setting will usually have its own paperwork or online forms to complete for risk assessments, and staff may need extra training to complete it.

Although it is not possible to remove all risks, the setting should show how they take steps to minimise them. According to the Health and

Safety Executive (HSE), there are five steps to a risk assessment, as shown in Figure 5.5.

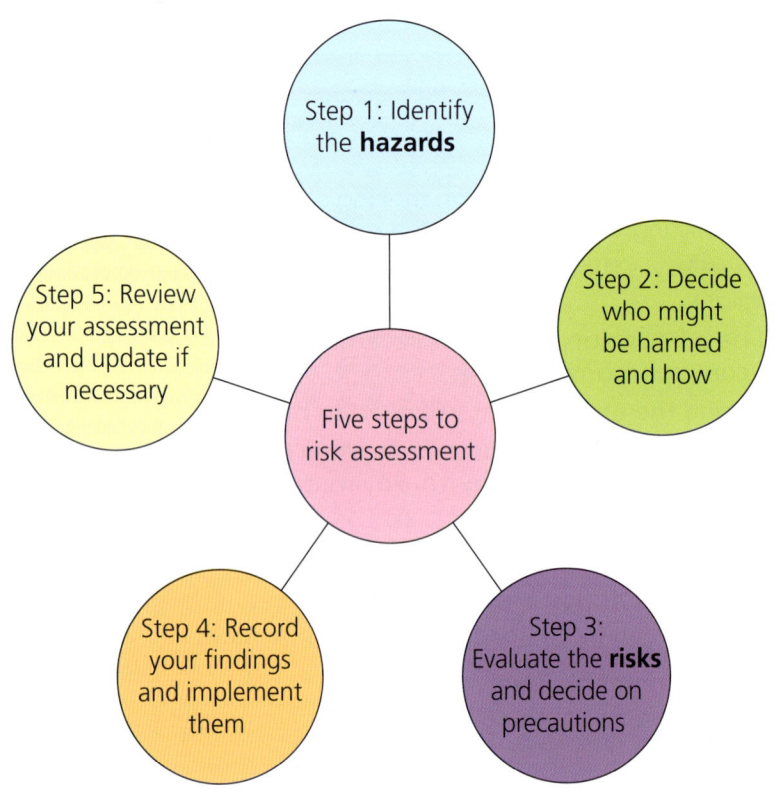

Five steps to risk assessment
- Step 1: Identify the **hazards**
- Step 2: Decide who might be harmed and how
- Step 3: Evaluate the **risks** and decide on precautions
- Step 4: Record your findings and implement them
- Step 5: Review your assessment and update if necessary

Figure 5.5 The five HSE steps to risk assessment

Activity

Look online for an example of an early years risk assessment form, such as this one from Torfaen County Borough Council:

www.torfaen.gov.uk/en/Related-Documents/Food,HealthandSafetyEnforcement/Health-and-Safety-at-Work/risk-assesment-template-for-nurserys-2015.pdf

Choose four types of risk on the form and look at the measures which the setting has put in place to reduce them.

Complete security checks during arrivals and departures

All staff and visitors have to sign in and out of the early years setting. This may be in a book, but for staff a digital pass is now more usual. Signing in and out is important so that it is known exactly who is in the building at any time. This information will be needed if there is a fire drill or emergency evacuation of the building.

Settings need to keep information about who will be bringing children to the setting and who will be collecting them. If someone different will be doing this, staff should be told about it in advance. Staff should never let

5 Legislation, policies and procedures in the early years

children leave the setting with a different person without contacting their parent or carer to authorise it.

Make sure equipment is safe to use

Before using any equipment, either indoors or outdoors, practitioners should always check that it is safe to use. This is particularly true of any electric or fire equipment: these should be checked regularly. Records will need to be kept showing that this has been done. Early years professionals should also ensure that all equipment complies with health and safety regulations. If you are going to use equipment with children for the first time, it is a good idea to practise using it beforehand, to be sure you know what to do.

> **Check what you know**
>
> How can settings ensure that they know who will be collecting children from the setting?

> **Extend**
>
> Find out about the kind of checks which need to be made on electrical and fire equipment. How often should they take place? Explain why these are important.

Follow the setting's procedures for first aid

The setting will have a first aid policy to list the procedures for first aid and for administering medicine and completing records. All settings need to have at least one person who is a paediatric first aider, available at all times when there are children in the setting and also to go with children on outings.

In many settings, all staff are trained in paediatric first aid. First aiders should receive training every three years to keep them up to date. Any staff who are not trained should be aware who the first aiders are and know how to contact them when needed. Parents should also be contacted if their child has been given first aid treatment or if they have had a head injury. They should always be informed in cases of more serious accidents or injuries, for example if an ambulance is needed.

> **Read and write**
>
> Using the most recent copy of the EYFS statutory guidance, make a list of the first aid requirements.

Ensure correct and hygienic hand washing, nappy changing and toileting routines are followed

Infections and germs can spread quickly in early years environments, as children are close together and may not yet understand the importance of good hygiene habits.

95

NCFE CACHE Level 1/2 Technical Award in Child Development and Care

One of the best ways of managing infection is for staff and children to wash their hands regularly.

- The setting should provide guidance to staff to ensure that the correct procedures are being used for hygienic hand washing, nappy changing and toileting routines.
- Staff should also show children the correct form of hand washing, and talk about why they should wash their hands after going to the toilet and before eating food.

HOW TO WASH YOUR HANDS

1. Apply soap on wet hands
2. Rub the palm of your hands
3. Don't forget the back!
4. Interlace your fingers
5. Rub thumbs
6. Pay attention to your nails and fingertips
7. Use water to rinse your hands
8. Dry with paper towel

Figure 5.6 Why is it important for everyone in early years settings to wash their hands regularly?

Safe disposal of bodily fluids and waste

All bodily fluids should be cleaned up immediately using paper towels and disinfectant, and staff should wear gloves and aprons to do this. In the case of larger spillages, floor mops should be rinsed using hot water and disinfectant or detergent.

Early years settings other than childminders and nannies are required to dispose of waste and bodily fluids separately. This will mean using separate indoor and outdoor bins for the following:

- nappies
- soiled paper towels
- anything which has been in contact with blood, faeces, vomit or urine.

5 Legislation, policies and procedures in the early years

The bins will usually be yellow so that they do not look the same as normal waste paper bins. They will also have lids on them to stop infections from spreading. Childminders or other home-based settings are also advised to keep separate bins for nappies and bodily waste for the same reason.

> **Read and write**
>
> Create a poster to explain what practitioners should do when disposing of bodily fluids and waste.

Report infectious diseases

As well as taking measures to stop the spread of infection, such as having hygiene processes and procedures, settings must make sure that they report any infectious diseases – sometimes known as **notifiable diseases**. These include:

- food poisoning
- hepatitis
- German measles
- measles
- mumps
- meningitis
- scarlet fever
- tuberculosis
- typhoid
- whooping cough.

The UK Health Security Agency requires that cases of these diseases are reported to the local authority so that the level of infection can be monitored.

When there is an infectious disease in the setting, the following steps are necessary:

- good ventilation
- more regular hand washing
- rigorous cleaning and disinfecting of items which are touched often.

Staff will also need to take extra care to clean and disinfect items which are used by babies and put in their mouths. Remember that:

- resources such as playdough may be a source of infection if children have not washed their hands
- other equipment which is often touched by children should be cleaned regularly.

> **Jargon buster**
>
> **Notifiable disease:** a disease which needs to be reported by law to the authorities.
>
> **Incident:** an event which might cause an injury or develop into an emergency.
>
> **Accident:** an unintended incident which might cause physical injury to a child, visitor or member of staff.

Report incidents and accidents

All **incidents** and **accidents** must be reported and recorded accurately in an incident or accident book. This is required by the EYFS statutory guidance, and serious accidents will also need to be reported to the HSE.

For accidents and incidents involving children, parents and carers need to be informed immediately. Ofsted will also need to be told about any serious accident, illness, injury or death of a child. The setting should have as much information as possible about what happened (see page 86 for more on RIDDOR).

> **Theory into practice**
>
> Tamara has just started to work in a nursery and is not yet first aid trained. She is in the outside area on a windy day when a piece of play equipment falls and hurts a child. She is the only adult outside and doesn't know who the first aider is or what to do.
> 1. Outline what Tamara should do and in what order.
> 2. Why is it important that she follows the correct procedure?

Follow emergency and fire evacuation procedures

Early years settings should have frequent **emergency** and fire evacuation practices so that all staff and children know what to do if necessary.

- A fire safety risk assessment should be carried out and kept up to date by the responsible person; this includes checking fire equipment and alarms, as well as making sure fire doors are kept clear and closed.
- Evacuation practices should take place at different times of the day so that all staff know what to do if there is an emergency at these times.
- When alarms go off, there should be guidance for checking toilets and quiet areas as well as outdoor areas and staff rooms. Although they should be held regularly, the EYFS does not specify how often.

> **Jargon buster**
>
> **Emergency:** a life-threatening situation or one which may pose immediate risk.

Carry out manual handling safely

The setting may have a manual handling policy to set out procedures which should be used by staff when lifting and moving equipment. This may have advice on posture and lifting positions as well as correct techniques.

> **Exam-style question**
>
> 2. What is the name of the person responsible for health and safety in early years settings?

Use of PPE

Staff in early years settings should be given PPE where it is needed, to stop infections and diseases from spreading. It should be normal procedure for PPE to be used where it is provided.

Early years settings are most likely to use disposable gloves and aprons. They should be worn whenever staff change a nappy or come into contact with bodily fluids, such as vomit or blood. They should always be removed straight after use, and hands should then be washed.

> **Check what you know**
>
> When should gloves and aprons be used as PPE?

Ensure food hygiene is maintained

Settings must make sure that they have good food hygiene to reduce the possibility of food poisoning, which can be very dangerous for young

5 Legislation, policies and procedures in the early years

children and babies. All early years practitioners who are preparing and serving food should have food hygiene training. This will include following safe procedures for washing, preparing, cooking and storing food.

Respond to dietary needs and requirements

Parents and carers will need to give information to early years settings about their child's dietary needs and requirements (see page 86 for more on RIDDOR). The EYFS statutory framework also states that the setting should obtain information about any food allergies, so that it is able to provide appropriate meals for children.

Follow off-site activities procedures

Although early years settings must think about the level of risk when taking children off site, according to the EYFS statutory guidance they do not necessarily need to complete a written risk assessment in every case. However, they must think about how they are managing risks and be able to show parents and inspectors how they do this.

Written assessments are up to individual settings. They should include a consideration of adult–child ratios and ensure that any vehicles have the correct insurance.

Theory into practice

You are taking a group of children for a walk to a local greengrocers as part of a topic on healthy eating. You have been asked to complete a risk assessment form, showing potential risks and the actions which should be taken to minimise them. Copy and complete the form below, assessing the types of risk which may occur. You can add more rows to the form if they are needed.

Risk Assessment Form			
Date:			
Activity	Potential risk and level (Scale of 1 to 5 where 1 is low and 5 is high)	Actions to be taken to minimise risk	Responsible person

Figure 5.7 A sample risk assessment form

> **Exam-style questions**
>
> 3 There is a serious outbreak of gastroenteritis in the setting. The nursery manager has called a meeting to discuss ways in which the spread of infection can be reduced.
>   a Outline what should be discussed at the meeting and the measures which should be taken.
>   b Explain the importance of doing this.
>   c Identify any further steps which the setting will need to take.

5.2.4 Equality and inclusion procedure

> **Five things to know ...**
>
> 1 All early years settings need to have procedures for equality, diversity and inclusion.
> 2 Equality means that everyone should be treated fairly and given equal opportunities.
> 3 Individual people's needs might have to be met in different ways.
> 4 Inclusion for early years means including the needs of every child in the setting.
> 5 Recognising diversity in the early years setting is important.

The terms **equality**, **diversity** and **inclusion** will be an important aspect of an early years practitioner's work with babies and children. You need to know what they mean as well as understand your responsibilities and the procedures for supporting each of them in your setting.

The policy you will need to refer to in your setting to find out about procedures is likely to be called the equality and diversity policy, or the equality, diversity and inclusion policy. (See also section 5.2.2.)

> **Jargon buster**
>
> **Equality:** individuals are treated in the same way.
>
> **Diversity:** the range of values, attitudes, cultures and beliefs held by different people.
>
> **Inclusion:** every child is given equal access to education and care.

Equality, diversity and inclusion policies often talk about removing 'barriers' so that everyone is included in activities. A barrier is something which stops an individual from taking part, and it can take different forms, as shown in Table 5.4.

5 Legislation, policies and procedures in the early years

Table 5.4 Potential barriers to inclusion

Type of barrier	Meaning
Physical	These may include barriers such as lack of access, for example: ■ no ramp for wheelchairs ■ no disabled toilets ■ no equipment to support communication. These barriers mean that some individuals will not be able to access the building, or in some cases the curriculum.
People's attitudes	Barriers caused by people's attitudes may include: ■ low expectations ■ lack of understanding or respect ■ discrimination ■ negative opinions. These may result in low self-esteem and low self-image.
Organisational	An organisational barrier could include a lack of provision through the EYFS curriculum and wider work of the setting so that children are not made aware of equality and diversity. It may also include inadequate policies or training so that staff are not sure how to act.

Figure 5.8 Why is it important for all staff to know about and understand equality and inclusion?

> **Check what you know**
>
> What does equality mean?

Equality

We looked briefly at equality legislation and procedure in section 5.2.2, and at the nine protected characteristics under the Equality Act 2010 in Figure 5.3. Everyone with these characteristics will need to be supported, and the setting should make sure that they are not treated unfairly. Some of the ways in which settings can do this are described below.

Provide resources that ensure all children can take part in every activity

Settings need to be inclusive to ensure that all babies and children are able to take part in activities. This means that those who have disabilities or other special educational needs will be given equal opportunities through the use of support or resources so that they can join in.

Make reasonable adjustments to activities so that all children have an equal chance to join in

Under the Equality Act 2010, **reasonable adjustments** may need to be made to activities so that all children can take part. Settings need to provide extra resources or training to ensure that they can do this.

Provide extra explanations so that everyone understands the rules of a game

If a child has communication difficulties or finds it more difficult to understand because of their age or needs, staff may need to provide more explanations so that the child can understand what is happening and what to do next.

> **Jargon buster**
>
> **Reasonable adjustment:** removing barriers and putting measures in place so that an individual can take part in an activity.

> **Theory into practice**
>
> A child aged three who has Type 1 diabetes will be starting at your nursery. This means that he will need to test his blood sugar level and then inject insulin regularly. The nursery have said that his parents will need to come in and do this when needed, as they do not have a member of staff who is trained to do it. They have also said that they have no experience of a child with diabetes.
>
> 1 Why is this not acceptable?
> 2 What is a reasonable adjustment in this situation?
> 3 Could the nursery take any further steps to support the child and his family?

Diversity

Diversity relates to the many differences between people. These may be related to values, cultures, attitudes and beliefs, and can also be physical.

5 Legislation, policies and procedures in the early years

Recognise and celebrate individual differences

All staff, including early years practitioners, should be able to recognise and celebrate difference. They should develop an awareness in children that everyone is different but that everyone is special.

Settings can use stories, dolls, positive role models and posters as well as a range of activities, such as role play. They can also celebrate difference, for example by highlighting things which are special about individuals through talking about them.

Activity

Think about the following:
- a child in the setting who has just celebrated Chinese New Year with her family
- a setting where one child is from an Afro-Caribbean background and all the other children are white
- a child who is **bilingual**
- a child who knows sign language as he has a parent who is deaf.

How might the setting use these as opportunities to celebrate individual differences?

Ensure dignity and respect

All babies and children should be treated with dignity and respect at all times. This means that others in the setting should make them feel valued. They should also be respected during nappy changing or where there is a need for **intimate care**. Information about babies and children should be kept confidential and their parents' wishes should be respected.

Ensure anti-discriminatory practice

Early years practitioners should ensure that the setting is a place where no form of discrimination is allowed. This means that staff should always challenge anyone who is discriminatory and report it, according to the equality and diversity policy.

Remember that children may discriminate without meaning to, and that adults can also have negative attitudes which they themselves are not aware of.

Jargon buster

Bilingual: speaking two languages.

Intimate care: when taking care of another person's personal care needs, for example when helping them to go to the toilet.

Theory into practice

Three girls are playing in the role play area when Raphael, one of the boys, asks if he can come in and play with them. You overhear the girls tell him that it is just a game for girls and tell him to go away.
1. What could you say to the girls?
2. Why is it important that they are challenged?

NCFE CACHE Level 1/2 Technical Award in Child Development and Care

> **Check what you know**
>
> What is meant by anti-discriminatory practice? How can settings ensure that everyone is treated with respect?

Provide positive images of all people within society

The setting should be able to show positive images of different people within society, through:

- displays
- books
- conversations with children
- inviting visitors who may have different characteristics from those which they have experienced.

Inclusion

We often use the term inclusion when we are talking about including children who have **special educational needs and disabilities (SEND)**. However, inclusion also means accepting, valuing and respecting everyone in the early years setting, whatever their background, ability or needs. All children are entitled to have whatever is needed to support their learning and development.

Provide access to appropriate resources and environment

All children should have access to the types of resources and an environment which are suitable for them. Through books, displays and other resources, the environment should reflect positive and diverse images of children from all backgrounds.

If children have additional needs which mean that they need further resources, the setting should be able to provide them; this also includes having more staff to provide support.

Make reasonable adjustments for physical or emotional needs

Practitioners might need to make reasonable adjustments so that children with physical or **emotional needs** can take part in activities. For example, some children are very sensitive to noise and this may upset them, so they might need to have a different space to carry out activities, or time out so that they can self-regulate. (See page 102 for an explanation of reasonable adjustments.)

> **Jargon buster**
>
> **Special educational needs and disabilities (SEND):** a learning need or disability which means that special support is needed to help a child or young person as part of inclusion.
>
> **Emotional needs:** conditions which need to be met to feel happy and fulfilled.
>
> **ADHD:** attention deficit hyperactivity disorder, a condition which affects behaviour and makes it difficult to concentrate.

> **Theory into practice**
>
> Maisie has just turned four. She is currently being assessed for **ADHD** and is impulsive: she finds it difficult to wait for her turn or sit quietly with a book, which can also make it harder for other children to concentrate on activities.
>
> Her behaviour has always been a cause for concern and so the setting has put a plan in place to help her while it waits for the assessment. Her key person has created a quiet space for her to go to and has developed some activities to work on with her if she finds the environment overwhelming.
>
> 1. What kinds of needs does Maisie have?
> 2. How has the setting made reasonable adjustments for her?
> 3. Why is this important?

5 Legislation, policies and procedures in the early years

Adapt materials and activities to meet the individual needs of the child and families/carers

Sometimes, early years practitioners might need to adapt or change materials and activities so that the child is able to take part and make progress at their own pace. For example:

- A child with communication needs might require more help to understand what they need to do.
- A throwing and catching activity might need to be changed to support a child who is unable to stand without help.

This is why it is important for all staff to know about the needs of the babies and children in their setting.

In some cases, it may also be necessary to give support to families and carers, for example if they speak **English as an additional language (EAL)** or have literacy needs which mean that they cannot read materials which are sent home. In each case, the setting needs to make sure that they communicate the information in another way.

Provide extra time for activity completion

Some children might need to have extra time to complete activities. For example, a young child who has medical needs might need to take more breaks from activities. Early years practitioners need to make sure that they allow for this when planning, so that all children are given the opportunity to achieve and develop in a way which is manageable for them.

Follow procedures to support children for whom English is an additional language (EAL)

Early years practitioners may also work with children who speak EAL. Table 5.5 shows two ways in which the child might be learning English.

Table 5.5 Two possible learning routes for children with EAL

Type of acquisition	Explanation
Simultaneous language learning	The child is bilingual because they have parents who speak a different language. They will be learning both languages at the same time, and will already be able to speak some English alongside another language.
Sequential language learning	This means that the child already speaks their home language fluently and has no knowledge of English. This could be because they have recently come to the UK but it can also be that English is not spoken at all at home. In both cases they will be unable to understand or speak any English at first.

Practitioners need to follow the setting's policy for supporting those who speak EAL. It is important to support children and encourage them to

> **Check what you know**
>
> Give an example of when a setting should adapt materials or activities to meet the individual needs of a child.

> **Jargon buster**
>
> **English as an additional language (EAL):** when someone speaks English but it is not their first language.

> **Check what you know**
>
> Give three examples of ways in which the setting can ensure that every child is given equal access to education and care.

NCFE CACHE Level 1/2 Technical Award in Child Development and Care

Jargon buster

Cultural identity: shared cultural characteristics, such as language, religion, festivals, music and food.

use their home language as much as possible, as this will help them to develop language skills in English. A child's **cultural identity** is also very important and this can be related to their languages.

The EAL policy should include using the following types of support:

- finding out about the child's language needs so that you can support them better
- working closely with parents and carers, and using interpreters if needed
- making sure the child's and parents' names are pronounced correctly
- continuing to talk to children, even if they are very quiet: it is normal for children to have a 'silent phase' when learning another language
- extending the child's speech where possible by asking them questions and modelling the correct form of language
- using stories with repetitive language.

Read and write

Oxfordshire County Council have produced some guidance on supporting children learning EAL in the early years. You can find it here:

www.oxfordshire.gov.uk/sites/default/files/file/working-early-years/eal_sen_booklet.pdf

Read through the guidance and look through some of the strategies suggested in Appendix 1 on page 14.

Create a leaflet to provide ideas and guidance for early years practitioners working with children who speak EAL.

Extend

The EYFS has a section on children whose home language is not English, under 'Learning and Development Considerations'. Find out what guidance is given and identify two things practitioners can do to support them.

Exam-style questions

4. Rhea and Nicolas are visiting the setting with their eight-month-old twins, Aisha and Iris. They are hoping that the children will be able to start there in the next few months. Both girls hear only Greek spoken in the home.
   a Outline what kind of measures the setting might put in place to support the girls and their parents.
   b Explain why it is important that staff in the setting know about the children's individual needs.

5.2.5 Safeguarding procedure

> **Five things to know …**
>
> 1. Safeguarding means protecting children and young people from harm.
> 2. Every setting will have a safeguarding policy and regular training for staff.
> 3. Safeguarding is the responsibility of all staff.
> 4. Every setting will have a DSL or designated safeguarding lead for reporting any concerns.
> 5. Staff should know about the different indicators of abuse and what to look for.

All early years settings have safeguarding procedures in place, and staff should have additional training so that they fully understand what to do. This is in line with the EYFS safeguarding and welfare requirements. Everyone should be aware of the signs of abuse and what to do if they have any concerns:

- They should use and follow the safeguarding policy.
- They should speak to the DSL.

Safeguarding

We looked at safeguarding in section 5.2.2 and the importance of all staff being aware of policies and procedures for protecting children. Safeguarding is the term used when we talk about keeping children safe from abuse or neglect. In this section we will learn about the different categories and indicators of abuse.

Protecting children from harm

Safeguarding is everyone's responsibility, and all early years practitioners should know about the correct procedures for keeping children safe from harm. As well as the setting's safeguarding policy, the EYFS statutory guidance gives information about what settings should do in cases of suspected abuse.

> **Activity**
>
> Using a copy of the EYFS statutory guidance, find out who settings should inform in cases of suspected abuse. In addition to the advice given, what documents does it suggest that practitioners refer to for additional information?

Categories and the indicators of abuse

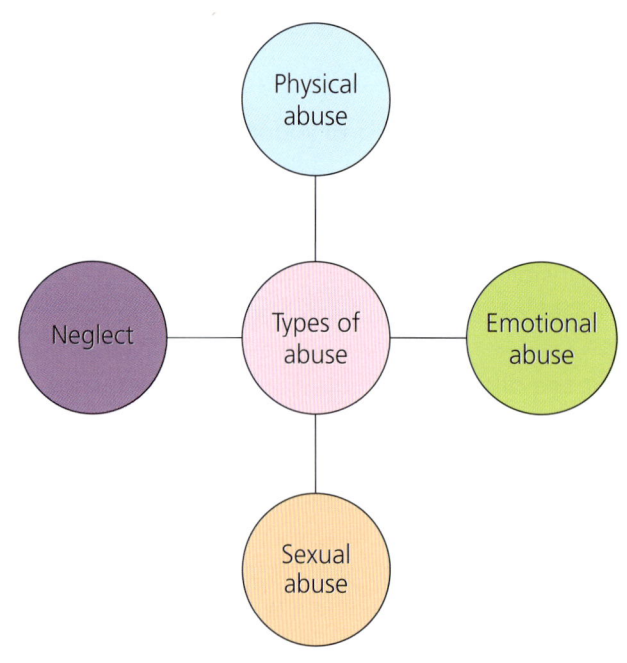

Figure 5.9 Types of abuse

Physical (someone deliberately harming a child's body)

Physical abuse can be difficult to identify, as all small children have bumps and bruises from time to time. However, it is important to look out for children who seem to have more injuries than usual. If staff are concerned about any physical injuries, they should keep a record of them with dates, in case they are needed at a later time.

- If bruising is seen on a regular basis, this may be a cause for concern.
- Fractures or broken bones should not happen very often, and should be noted by staff.
- Any kind of burn should be monitored, as these should be very rare, if seen at all in young children.

Early years practitioners should also note if children flinch or react unusually when adults move suddenly or go towards them, or if they try to cover up any injuries. Regular absences or reported illnesses can also be a sign of physical abuse.

Emotional (constant verbal insults, ridiculing, mocking)

Emotional abuse can also be difficult to identify, as it may happen over an extended period and usually takes place in the home. Children may be told that they are worthless or regularly mistreated or insulted in a way that affects their emotional development. It can be very frightening and traumatic for them. In some cases, it takes place alongside other forms of abuse.

> **Check what you know**
>
> Name three types of physical abuse.

5 Legislation, policies and procedures in the early years

Emotional abuse can have the following impact on the child:

- Low self-esteem: emotional abuse is likely to cause low self-esteem as the child will feel worthless and unloved. They may also go back to behaviour which is usually shown by a younger child, such as having toilet 'accidents', thumb sucking or attention seeking.
- Withdrawn social behaviour: children might withdraw from activities and from playing with others as they lose confidence. They might also be reluctant to leave the setting at the end of a session with the adult who is carrying out the abuse.
- Stammering and stuttering: these can often be a sign of anxiety, and can be caused by emotional abuse.

Sexual (inappropriate sexual contact, involvement or behaviour harming a child)

Sexual abuse means the forcing of sexual behaviour on a baby or child. It also includes making a child look at pornographic material. Some of the signs of sexual abuse might be:

- Bruises in genital areas: this is unlikely to be caused by an accident.
- Pain in genital areas: the child may seem uncomfortable, or touch their genital area often, particularly if they are sore or have been infected.
- Sudden change in behaviour: the child might become clingy to adults in the setting or not want to leave with a familiar adult. They might seem to be anxious and upset. They might also show signs of sexualised behaviour or talking in a way which is not expected at a young age.

Extend

The NSPCC has some stories of abuse on this webpage, and how it has affected different children and young people:

www.nspcc.org.uk/what-is-child-abuse/childrens-stories/

Use these examples or research your own to write an extended account of how different forms of abuse will affect a child in the long term. How can adults take steps to support them and help them to move on?

Neglect (not providing for or meeting a child's needs)

Neglect is a form of abuse as it means that the child's basic needs are not being met by those who should be caring for them. It can be easier to notice than other forms of abuse as the child might come into the setting unwashed, hungry or with poor general hygiene. Parents and carers might not reply when the setting asks them for information or support.

Neglect will affect the child's physical and emotional development. Indicators of neglect include:

- Untreated illness: the child is regularly unwell and is not receiving enough medical attention.

NCFE CACHE Level 1/2 Technical Award in Child Development and Care

Jargon buster

Confidentiality: making sure that private information about children and their families is kept private.

Privileged information: information which should only be given to authorised people.

All early years practitioners need to know about and understand the importance of **confidentiality** as part of their role. They will work with many babies and children, and so will be given **privileged information** about them and their families including addresses, health and other personal information which may be sensitive. This information should not be shared with anyone who does not need to know it.

Why confidentiality must be maintained

Confidentiality must be maintained for several reasons, as shown in Figure 5.11.

Maintaining confidentiality:
- Builds trust between all those caring for the child
- Safeguards the child, parents and family
- Respects privacy
- Is a legal requirement

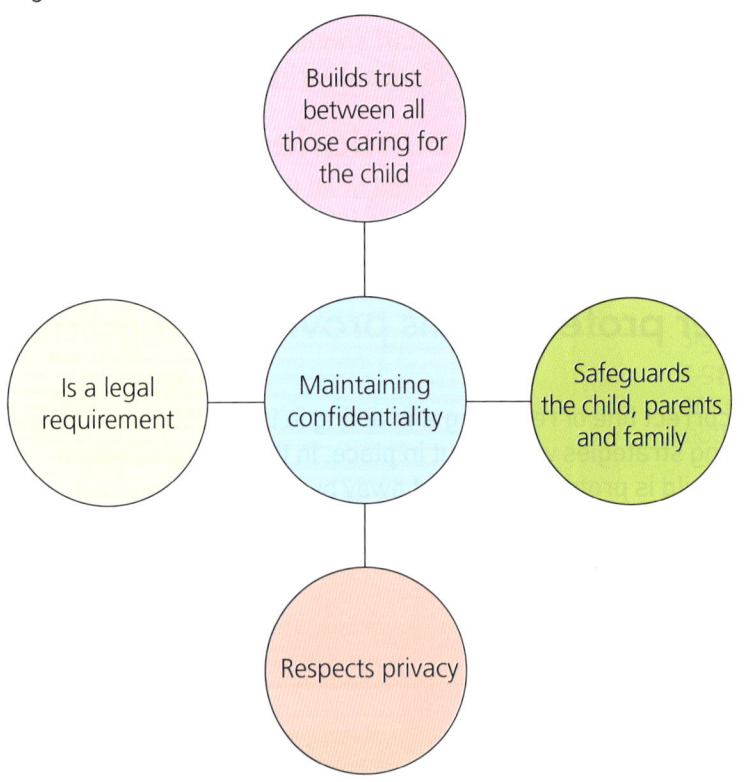

Figure 5.11 Reasons for maintaining confidentiality

It builds trust between all those caring for the child

The relationship between early years practitioners and parents is important, as it will be one of the first relationships parents have with professionals about their child.

- A policy of confidentiality helps families and professionals to build a feeling of trust and understanding with one another.
- It also means that they will be able to share information freely without worrying that it will be given to other people.

In some cases, families might need to be asked about whether information they are giving is confidential, or whether it can be passed on to others.

5 Legislation, policies and procedures in the early years

It safeguards the child, parents and family

The wellbeing of the child, parents and family is important and is at the heart of the work of early years practitioners. Not maintaining confidentiality may put children and families at risk if others find out about it.

> **Theory into practice**
>
> Maya and her daughter Dora have relocated to the area as Maya was a victim of domestic violence. They have been rehoused in a nearby refuge and Dora is starting to attend the early years setting. Maya has told the setting about her situation so that they can support Dora, but has asked for reassurance that this information is kept confidential, and only given to those members of staff who need to know about it.
>
> 1. Why is it important to keep Maya and Dora's information confidential?
> 2. How else will maintaining confidentiality support Maya and Dora?

It is a legal requirement

Maintaining confidentiality is a legal requirement under GDPR. Everyone must be aware that they should keep any personal information about staff, children and families private. This should mean that written records are locked away or password-protected, and that staff do not talk about anything which is confidential when they are out of the setting. (For more on GDPR and confidentiality, see section 5.2.2.)

It respects privacy

Having a culture of confidentiality ensures that the privacy of children and families is respected. As well as having access to personal information, the setting will need to be aware of any challenging situations or circumstances which the family are going through, as this is likely to affect the child and their behaviour. This type of information should not be given to everyone.

> **Activity**
>
> Think about the following situations and outline what should have happened to meet confidentiality procedures:
>
> - Two colleagues on the bus are talking about work and have been discussing one of the children and her family. Another man on the bus speaks to them as they get off and says that he knows the child's parents.
> - An early years practitioner is preparing for a meeting and has photocopied some sensitive information including children's names to circulate as part of her presentation.
> - A safeguarding situation has arisen and the member of staff who is concerned has spoken to several people before going to the DSL.
> - A student has prepared a leaflet for new parents as part of her course and has included photos of children in the setting without obtaining parents' permission.

> **Check what you know**
>
> Give three reasons why confidentiality must be maintained.

> **Jargon buster**
>
> **Breach:** failing to keep to an agreement.

Role of the early years practitioner

The early years practitioner's role means that they need to know when confidentiality must be maintained and when there might be a reason to **breach** confidentiality rules.

Maintain confidentiality

In most cases, confidentiality will need to be maintained and the correct procedures followed for doing this. This will include:

- Obtaining consent and permission: parents and carers need to give their consent or permission if any information about their child, including photographs, is going to be passed on to others.
- Ensuring secure handling and storage: settings need to make sure that all recorded information is kept securely and handled carefully.
- Sharing information: information should be shared only with those who need to know.

Breach confidentiality

In some cases, it may be necessary to breach, or break, confidentiality rules. Table 5.6 explains the reasons why this might need to happen.

Table 5.6 Reasons for breaching confidentiality

Reason it is necessary to break confidentiality rules	Explanation
To protect a child	This may happen in cases where a child will be put at more risk if confidentiality is maintained, for example if they are at risk of harm or abuse.
To whistleblow	This means that a member of staff, volunteer or student is suspected of **malpractice**, such as behaving inappropriately or breaking the law. Another member of staff might need to bring this to the setting's attention. There is likely to be a **whistleblowing** policy, which sets out what should be done in this situation to keep children safe.
The 'need to know' principle	In situations where there has been malpractice, it might be necessary to share information which is normally confidential so that a person can be brought to justice.

> **Jargon buster**
>
> **Malpractice:** failing to carry out professional duties.
>
> **Whistleblowing:** when someone in an organisation reports malpractice or wrongdoing, sometimes to authorities outside of the setting.

> **Check what you know**
>
> When is it necessary to breach confidentiality rules?

> **Extend**
>
> Research early years whistleblowing policies to find out why they are necessary and what measures settings should have in place.

5 Legislation, policies and procedures in the early years

Test your knowledge

1. What does legislation mean?
2. Give **three** aspects of Ofsted's role.
3. Explain the difference between policy and procedure.
4. Give **four** examples of protected characteristics under the Equality Act 2010.
5. What is involved in a risk assessment?
6. How does the EYFS statutory guidance identify what settings should do to support children's rights?
7. Name **three** ways in which settings can maintain health and safety in the setting.
8. How can settings show that they support equality, diversity and inclusion?
9. Describe what is meant by safeguarding.
10. When might it be necessary to breach confidentiality?

Assignment practice

Case study

Sandy and David have two children in the setting, Sammy, aged two, and Leah, aged four. Leah was born with spina bifida and has significant physical needs, including the support of an assistant to help her with toileting and moving around using her walker. As a result, the family have had a number of meetings in the setting with different health professionals, such as a physiotherapist, alongside early years staff.

There is to be a meeting between staff at the setting and the primary school where Leah will be starting in a few months' time so that they can prepare for her arrival. There will be several people attending and each will be writing a report about Leah and her needs so that they can share information and support her transition to school.

Task

1. Write a report for the meeting which sets out how the setting has ensured that Leah has been treated in an inclusive way and the kinds of adjustments which have been made. This will include details of how the setting has:
   - made sure that Leah has physical access
   - met Leah's toileting needs
   - ensured that Leah is able to participate in all activities.

   You should also consider what risk assessments might be needed.

2. Name the legislation and policies which the setting has taken into consideration when making provision for Leah.

3. Describe the kind of issues which Leah might face when she first starts school and how these barriers can be overcome.

6 Expectations of the early years practitioner

About this content area

This unit is about understanding professional expectations around appearance, behaviour and other aspects of your role. As well as knowing what these expectations are, you will need to know why each of them is important. Your setting is likely to have a staff code of conduct which will set these out and also explain other staff responsibilities.

6.1 Appearance
6.2 Behaviour
6.3 Attendance and punctuality

6.1 Appearance

Five things to know …

1. Dress in a safe and professional way for work.
2. Remember that you are a role model.
3. Be respectful to others.
4. Think about practicalities.
5. Be aware of your setting's policy on appearance.

Although it is important to be able to express ourselves as individuals, how you look also plays an important part in creating a good impression to others and showing that you are professional. Many of the expectations for appearance will be requirements of the setting's policies.

Expected appearance

All those who work in early years environments need to know what is expected around their appearance. It is important for staff to have the same approach, so that the needs of the babies and children in their care can be met. Staff policies, such as the dress code or uniform policy, set out what is acceptable in the setting and the reasons behind this. (For more on policies and procedures see Unit 5.)

6 Expectations of the early years practitioner

- Clean hair, tied back if long
- Remove jewellery/piercings if unsafe
- Clean skin and clothing
- Short, clean nails
- Covered body art
- Safe clothing (flat shoes, respectful, practical for indoors and outdoors)

Figure 6.1 Early years practitioners are required to follow these guidelines on their appearance

Good personal hygiene

Early years workers must have a good approach to personal hygiene:

- Babies and children are more vulnerable to infections as they do not have a fully developed immune system.
- Adults are also likely to pick up infections more regularly when they start working with babies and children; illnesses and infections can spread quickly in early years environments.

Regular hand washing will reduce the chance of picking up coughs, colds and other infections. This is likely to be part of the setting's health and safety policy (see Unit 5). Practitioners are also role models for children, who copy what they see adults doing.

Clean hair, tied back (if long)

Hair should always be kept clean and neat in the setting. This is because those who work in early years will be carrying out a range of different duties and will have close contact with children.

Practical to allow for movement, and for wearing indoors and outdoors

As well as being smart and comfortable, clothes should allow for movement and be appropriate for the weather as early years practitioners will be spending time outside with children.

Shoes should be flat as you might need to move quickly to help a child or prevent a hazard; it also means that you are less likely to trip over. It might be sensible to have a change of shoes and warm, waterproof coats and boots to make sure you are ready to go outside in all weathers!

Respectful, without offensive or disrespectful slogans or too much skin revealed

You should not wear T-shirts or other clothes bearing slogans which might offend someone. If you are in any doubt about something, it is best not to wear it and choose something plain. Clothes which are ripped, such as jeans, are not likely to be permitted, and those which reveal too much skin should also be avoided.

> **Activity**
>
> Design an illustrated leaflet for new staff with information about their appearance in the setting. Remember to also include information about hair, nails, jewellery, piercings and body art. It may help you to look online at staff policies from other early years settings. (Refer also to Unit 5, which is about policies and procedures in the early years.)

Meet uniform requirements and the setting's policies

If you are asked to wear a uniform, this should be mentioned at interview so that you know about it in advance. Uniforms usually have the setting's logo on them and can look very smart.

Always check your setting's policy to make sure that you know the rules when choosing clothing to wear to work (see Unit 5).

> **Read and write**
>
> Make a list of five things which you should remember when planning what to wear in early years settings.

> **Exam-style question**
>
> 1 Which of these is *not* usually a requirement for early years practitioners?
>   a Short fingernails
>   b Long hair tied back
>   c No make up
>   d Covering most tattoos and body art

6 Expectations of the early years practitioner

6.2 Behaviour

Five things to know ...

1 Know about and read your setting's policies.
2 Make sure you always remain professional.
3 Communicate effectively with others.
4 Remain positive.
5 Be aware of health and safety practices.

When thinking about behaviour, all staff should be aware of their impact on others in the work environment. The important thing to remember is that practitioners are there for the children, and that being cheerful, respectful and kind to others will also show them how to behave.

Work within the policies and procedures of the setting to meet legislation

Carry out health, safety and hygiene practices

All settings have a responsibility to keep children safe. They also have to follow the Health and Safety at Work Act 1974, which gives guidance around health and safety.

This means that settings will have set routines and practices for health, safety and hygiene. These should be a part of any staff **induction** and included in the health and safety policy so that everyone knows what is expected of them.

The setting should also have a member of staff who is responsible for health and safety, so that staff know who to speak to if they have any concerns. (For more detail about health and safety procedures, see Unit 5, section 5.2.3.)

Everyone in the setting is responsible for keeping children safe, and the policy will cover a range of procedures and practices which all staff should know about. The main health, safety and hygiene practices should include:

- risk assessment
- health and safety routines.

Risk assessment

This process is about identifying and preventing risks. Most settings carry out written risk assessments for activities, resources and areas

Jargon buster

Induction: the process of introducing new staff to the setting.

that are often used. Early years practitioners should also be aware of possible risks in different situations.

(For more detail on risk assessments, see Unit 5, section 5.2.3.)

Health and safety routines

- Cleaning: regular cleaning of the setting including toilets, toys and other resources is important to stop bacteria and viruses from spreading. Toys which are used by babies should be sterilised regularly, as they are likely to have been put in their mouths. Any equipment which is used for babies should also be sterilised using an appropriate method.
- Food hygiene: any area of the setting that is used for food and drink will need to be thoroughly cleaned. This will include highchairs and tables as well as beakers, plates and cutlery. When food is prepared, the work surfaces, chopping boards and anything being used to prepare food will also need to be kept clean. There are rules in place to make sure that food is stored or cooked at the right temperatures; this is to stop any outbreaks of food poisoning.
- Checking all areas regularly: early years workers need to be aware of health and safety at all times, particularly at the beginning of the day. This includes making sure that equipment is safe and that there are no visible hazards. Outdoor areas in particular should be regularly checked for litter, animal mess and any damage to fences or gates.
- Home time: settings will have routines in place to make sure that children are kept safe when it is time to go home. Children will usually be handed over to their parent or carer in a gated area or indoors. If someone different is collecting their child, the setting should be informed in advance so that they are prepared for this.

Activity

Using the internet, type in the words 'health and safety policy nursery'.

What can you find in the policies? What types of topics are covered?

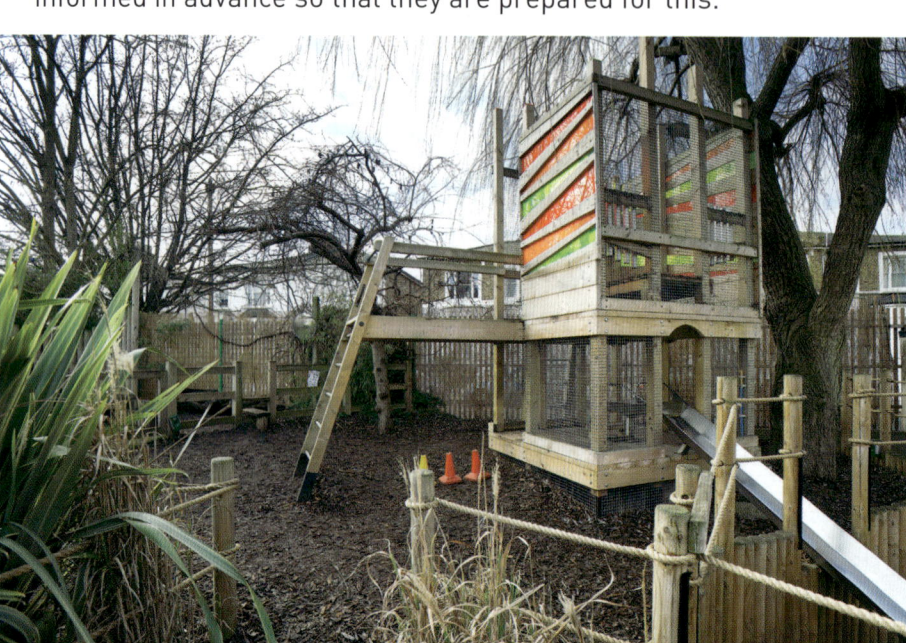

Figure 6.2 Why are outdoor areas checked at the start of a session?

6 Expectations of the early years practitioner

Show respect and maintain the children's and parents' dignity

All adults in the setting should show respect towards other staff and children and to those who visit, including parents and carers. This means that they should be approachable and friendly.

If the practitioner needs to speak to parents or carers about something confidential, they should find a quiet and private room to do this.

Staff should never speak negatively or gossip about others when outside the setting, particularly about children and families who are in their care. It is important to always be respectful and considerate of children and their families. From the point of view of other staff, it is also much easier to work with someone who is trustworthy and positive, smiles and greets others, and offers to help.

Dress code

As we have already discussed in section 6.1, it is important for practitioners to make sure they follow their setting's policies and procedures around their dress code (see also Unit 5).

Maintain professional boundaries

Boundaries are important and should be part of the way you behave and work when in the setting. They mean that you should always act in a professional way, and this includes reporting any concerns to your line manager or the designated safeguarding lead (DSL) if these are around safeguarding. Some examples of appropriate **professional boundaries** are given below. If you are not sure what this means, look at other adults and how they behave or talk to your line manager. Remember you are there to support children's learning and development as well as the work of your colleagues. (For more on roles and responsibilities in early years settings, see Unit 7.)

Jargon buster

Professional boundaries: the limit of a relationship in a professional situation.

Appropriate relationships

All relationships within the setting should be appropriate, which means that they should stay professional, even for volunteers on placement.

There should be professional boundaries around the way in which adults communicate with one another in the setting: having professional boundaries means that relationships should not be too personal, such as asking colleagues for personal advice or discussing personal issues with them.

There should also be boundaries around the type of language you use with colleagues; for example, you should not swear or use inappropriate expressions with them.

Maintain confidentiality

All staff should know about and understand confidentiality. This means that any information which they have about others as part of their role should remain private, and only those who need to know should be given this information.

Settings will have a confidentiality policy to make sure that all staff understand this issue. (For more on policies and procedures, see Unit 5.)

> **Activity**
>
> Find an example of an early years confidentiality policy online. Note down what it says about:
> - how information is stored in the setting
> - when to share information with parents.

Use of mobile phones

In most early years settings, personal mobile phones belonging to staff need to be switched off and stored in a secure place during the day. This is because they are a distraction when staff are supervising babies and children, and because cameras on phones should never be used in the setting. This is for safeguarding reasons.

Personal mobile phones might be needed when staff are on trips to contact others in emergencies, but cameras on phones should not be used – the setting will provide its own device for this. It is important that parents are also aware of this if they volunteer in the setting or on a trip.

> **Theory into practice**
>
> Mayuri is taking a group of children to a local farm and has three parent helpers with her. She has provided them with notes about what to look for and questions to ask the children when they are with the animals. She has also given them all her phone number so that they can contact her if they need to during the trip.
>
> At lunchtime she notices one of the parents taking photos of a group of children and politely asks her not to, but the parent replies that she should be able to take pictures of her own child, who is in her group.
>
> 1. How could this situation have been avoided?
> 2. What could Mayuri do to ensure that parents are more aware of the setting's policy and why it is important?

Use of social media

Although staff can have social media for their own personal use, this should not be done within the setting environment. It is also important that they do not contact or make connections on social media with parents or allow them to follow them. This is because it will be difficult to keep professional boundaries in this situation.

Parents may have their own groups or pages to communicate with one another, but staff should not be part of this and should be contacted

6 Expectations of the early years practitioner

through the setting. (Most settings will have a social media or e-safety policy. For more on policies, see Unit 5.)

Positive attitude

Early years staff should think about how they come across to others, both to babies and children in the setting and to other adults. Having a positive attitude means that you act as a positive role model and professional practitioner. Figure 6.3 shows the different elements to creating a positive attitude.

> **Check what you know**
>
> Can you be friends with parents outside the setting and on social media? Give reasons for your answer.
>
> What policies should you look at to find out about the use of mobile phones in the setting?

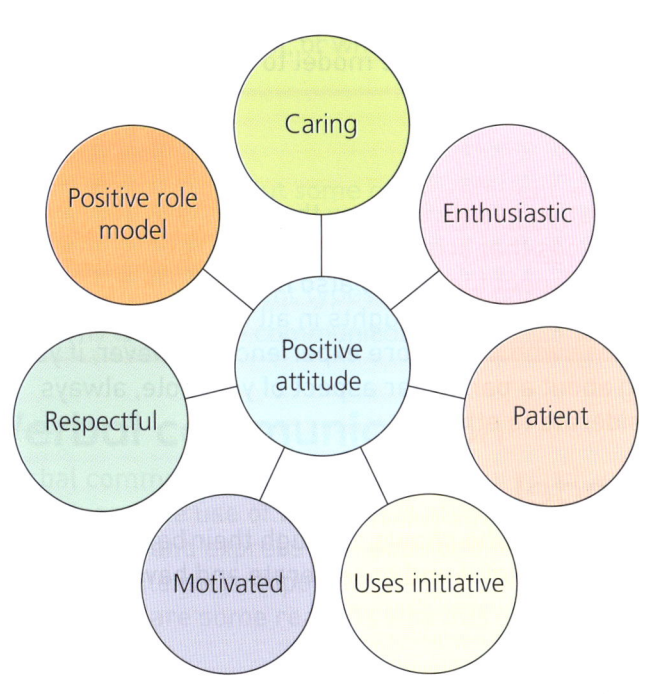

Figure 6.3 Practitioners can show others that they have a positive attitude in different ways

Elements surrounding "Positive attitude": Caring, Enthusiastic, Patient, Uses initiative, Motivated, Respectful, Positive role model

Patient

Patience is essential when you are working with young children. They will need more time to process information when you are talking to them, so you may need to give them longer to answer. They may also become easily upset or frustrated by the actions of others and need adults to help them by understanding their feelings and talking things through with them. Working in an early years environment means you will also need to be flexible and give others the time that they need in the workplace.

Uses initiative

Using your initiative means being able to see what needs to be done without being told to do it, for example moving something out of the way which may be a health and safety hazard or checking the toilets if it is time for a story to make sure everyone is ready and can join in. It also

> **Extend**
>
> Look at The Communication Trust website:
>
> www.thecommunicationtrust.org.uk
>
> Find the booklet 'Universally Speaking', which sets out some of the expectations for children's speech and language from birth to five years.
> - What can you find out about how to encourage communication in babies?
> - What should most young children be able to do using language by the age of three years?
> - What should you do if you have any worries about a child's speech and language development?

Use clear language

Always be clear in what you say and how you say it. This is important with both adults and children, and if it is something important, it is worth asking them to repeat it back to you to check their understanding.

Young children will not be able to take on too much information at once, so it is important to keep sentences simple. Adults also exaggerate their facial expressions and tone of voice to help children understand what they are talking about.

Appropriate for the situation

Always think about the situation or circumstances when communicating with others:

- Your language when talking to colleagues or parents will be more formal than when you are speaking to a young child.
- You might also need to change the way you communicate to meet the needs of others. For example, if you are talking to a person who has a hearing impairment, make sure that you are facing them so that they can read your facial expressions and lipread if necessary.

Non-verbal communication

Non-verbal communication takes place by using **visual cues**. This means passing on information in a way which is different from speech.

You can communicate non-verbally through the use of gestures, body language, touch, facial expressions, labels or symbols, and by making sure that you actively listen to what the other person is saying.

> **Check what you know**
>
> When do you use verbal communication? What does it help you to communicate to others?

> **Jargon buster**
>
> **Visual cues:** clues to help pass on messages or information, such as pointing to something as you are talking about it.

> **Activity**
>
> Think about how you might communicate the following to children using non-verbal communication:
> - 'Can you come here?'
> - 'Well done!'
> - 'Come and sit down next to me.'
> - 'It's time to listen.'
> - 'Let's do your coat up.'

6 Expectations of the early years practitioner

Active listening

It is important to actively listen and to show that you are giving your attention to what others are saying. You can do this by:

- looking at them as they are speaking
- using different facial expressions
- acknowledging what they are saying
- being physically at the same level as young children when talking to them.

Sensitive and respectful

Always be sensitive to others when communicating with them, and be kind. You might not always know if something is upsetting or worrying them, or if they are feeling unwell. Offer to speak to them at another time if it is not convenient.

Body language

Body language allows you to communicate your feelings and what you are doing. This form of non-verbal communication also shows your level of interest in what others are saying.

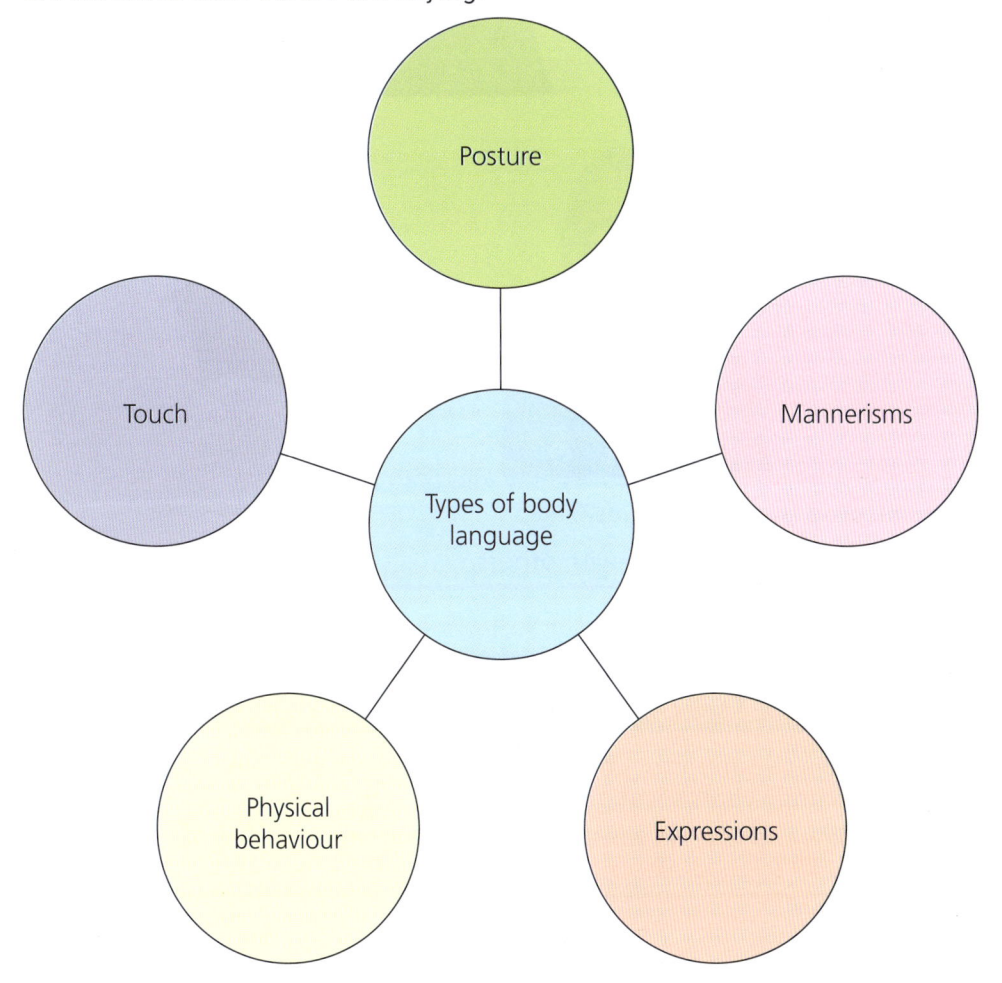

Figure 6.4 Different types of body language

Body language can be positive or negative, and others will pick up on it when communicating with you:

- A tense or anxious person might have hunched shoulders and poor posture, or folded arms and an unhappy expression.
- Someone who is more relaxed might look more approachable and be smiling.

Activity

Figure 6.5 What is being communicated by these images?

Give three examples of ways in which we communicate with others.

Exam-style questions

2 Explain the importance of being professional as a member of staff in an early years setting.
3 Outline the ways in which you can do this, and identify some of the benefits to children.

6 Expectations of the early years practitioner

6.3 Attendance and punctuality

Five things to know …

1. Be as reliable as you can.
2. Always tell the setting as soon as you can if you cannot be present.
3. Make sure you are always on time for work.
4. Take breaks at the correct times and return on time.
5. Book personal appointments in your own time.

Attendance

Your setting will have expectations for attendance for all staff, and it will be part of your role to make sure that you keep to these. Through regular attendance, you will develop positive relationships with other staff as they will know that they can trust you to be there for mutual support. Attendance is part of being professional and is important for the reasons listed in Table 6.1.

Table 6.1 Effects of good attendance at work

Effect of good attendance at work	Why is this important?
Meet adult–child ratios	Early years settings are legally obliged to have specific age-related adult–child ratios. The ratios are there to make sure that the children's needs can be met and that they are kept safe and secure. If members of staff do not come to work, the adult–child ratios will be affected.
Keep children safe	The correct number of adults in the setting will also mean that children are supervised correctly and are kept safe. Very young children are not aware of danger, and need to be watched by adults for much of the time.
Parents and carers can rely on the early years setting to care for their child	Parents and carers, who in many cases are paying for childcare, need to be able to trust the setting to care for their child. If there are not enough adults to care for and watch the number of babies and children, parents and carers will not be able to rely on the setting.
Meet children's needs	There should be enough adults in the setting to meet individual children's needs. This includes making sure that they have food and sleep when needed, as well as meeting their learning and developmental needs. If children have SEND, more staff will need to be employed to help support their needs.

> ### Activity
>
> Using the latest EYFS statutory guidance, find out the ratios required for the following (other than childminders):
> - children aged under two years
> - children aged two years
> - children aged three years and over in maintained nursery schools and nursery classes.
>
> What does the guidance say about including in the ratios 16- and 17-year-olds who are on placement?

Figure 6.6 Why does staff attendance mean that parents can rely on the setting to care for their child?

How to deal with attendance issues

Attendance is important and showing that you are trustworthy and reliable is part of your role. The other staff need to know that you will be there each day and can support them as well as the children. However, there will always be times when you are not able to attend, and you should follow these guidelines to avoid causing further problems.

Inform your manager if you are unable to attend due to illness

You should always let your manager know as soon as you can if you are not able to attend the setting. This will give them the maximum amount of time to find other staff to cover for you.

6 Expectations of the early years practitioner

Book personal appointments outside work time

If you need to visit the doctor, hospital or dentist, you should try to book these types of appointments outside work time. In some cases this may not be possible, but the setting should have as much notice as possible.

Show reliability by keeping to agreed work patterns

Make sure you know when you are supposed to be in the setting, particularly if you work different hours or shifts. If you need to, double-check rotas regularly to be sure, and set yourself reminders. This is important so that others can see you are reliable.

> **Check what you know**
>
> List three ways that you can make sure any attendance issues are avoided.

Punctuality

Punctuality means being on time. All staff and volunteers are required to arrive at work on time: this shows that you are professional and are able to plan ahead and organise yourself. You will need to leave home at a set time each day to be sure that you arrive at the setting on time.

Table 6.2 shows the effect of punctuality on the setting.

Table 6.2 The effects of punctuality on the setting

Effect of punctuality	Why is this important?
The early years setting can open safely	When staff can be relied on to be punctual, it ensures that the setting has enough staff to set up and open safely with the right number of adults. If managers have unreliable staff, it will be much more difficult to plan safely.
Activities are ready for the children when they arrive	Early years practitioners need to arrive in good time so that activities can be set up. The learning environment will be ready for the children when they arrive, and all the resources and equipment will have been checked.
Effective teamwork can take place	Arriving on time shows that you respect other members of staff and their time. If you are regularly late or do not attend, you will be putting pressure on them and raising their stress levels. It also implies that you do not value them as colleagues. A team of people who trust one another and can rely on what they say will run smoothly and have high morale.
Children are well cared for and their needs are met	Where staff are punctual and reliable, and the team get on well and respect one another, children are more likely to be well cared for. This is because the staff are better prepared for what they should be doing.

Ways to maintain expected timekeeping

You should always maintain the expected timekeeping of the setting, even if you are on a placement. This is because staff will rely on you: they have planned for you to be there and will be expecting you. You should always:

- arrive on time at the start of the day
- return on time after a break
- finish at the agreed time at the end of the day.

Theory into practice

Jamal has been volunteering in an early years setting as part of his apprenticeship. He has been punctual for most of the time he has been there, but for the past couple of weeks he has started to arrive later and later.

1. What effect might this have on the rest of the team?
2. Is there anything else that his poor timekeeping might influence?
3. What should happen next?

Exam-style questions

4. Andy has been working at the setting for two years. He arrives early every morning to help set up and always has a smile. He uses his initiative and goes out of his way to help others. His enthusiasm and caring nature are clearly visible. Other staff regularly comment on his positive outlook and say that he is very easy to work with.
   a. Outline why Andy is a popular member of staff.
   b. Discuss how his positive attitude will help him and others to carry out their roles effectively.
   c. Analyse what effect this will have on the children in the setting.

Test your knowledge

1. Why is appearance important for early years practitioners?
2. Why should long hair be tied back?
3. What should early years practitioners do if they have piercings or body art?
4. What type of clothes should be worn in an early years setting and why?
5. Give two examples of health and safety practices which should be followed in an early years setting.
6. What does 'professional boundaries' mean?
7. Can mobile phones be used in early years settings?
8. Explain the importance of confidentiality in an early years setting.
9. Give two examples of verbal and two of non-verbal communication.
10. Why is punctuality important for effective teamwork?

6 Expectations of the early years practitioner

Assignment practice

Case study

An early years setting is about to advertise for the role of an early years assistant. You have been asked to help to write a person specification. The form has the format shown below:

Early years assistant: Person specification		
	Essential	Desirable
Skills, knowledge, experience		
Personal qualities		
Qualifications		

Task

1 Using bullet points, copy and complete the middle section of the form in both columns (Essential and Desirable) under the heading 'Personal qualities'.

2 Evaluate the importance of each one, and justify why you have chosen it.

135

7 Roles and responsibilities within early years settings

About this content area

You will come into contact with a range of different roles and responsibilities in early years settings. Some of the people you work with will be external to the setting, while others will be part of your team. You will need to know about these roles and how you can work in partnership with them to support babies and children.

7.1 Early years practitioner roles
7.2 Partnership working in the early years
  7.2.1 How partnership working benefits the child, family and early years practitioner
7.3 Specialist roles within early years settings
7.4 Specialist roles outside early years settings

7.1 Early years practitioner roles

Five things to know …

1. All early years practitioners have a wide range of roles in the setting.
2. There will also be staff in the setting who have additional responsibilities.
3. The number of staff with different roles will depend on the type of setting.
4. All roles include keeping children safe, supporting children's development and working in partnership with others.
5. Staff also work with professionals from outside the setting.

You will need to understand the general roles and responsibilities of those working in early years settings. (See also Unit 4, section 4.3 for information on types of early years setting.)

Table 7.1 outlines the different job titles and roles in early years settings.

7 Roles and responsibilities within early years settings

Table 7.1 A summary of the different roles in early years settings

Job title	Role
Manager/person in charge of setting	The manager or person in charge is responsible for everything within the setting. They need to ensure that the children and families who come to the setting are being cared for and supported. Their responsibilities also include staffing, budgets, health and safety, safeguarding, and setting policies and procedures.
Early years practitioner	The early years practitioner (or EYP) is a designated occupational role within the early years workforce. They will be qualified at Level 2 in early years care and education. They have a range of responsibilities as part of their role, including meeting care routines, working with parents and carers, liaising with other professionals, observing and planning, and developing effective interactions with children.
Room leader	An experienced practitioner is responsible for running a room within the setting; for example, a baby room for young children or a pre-school room with children of three and four years.
Key person	A member of staff in an early years setting who gets to know and works closely with a designated group of children and their families.
Childminder	A childminder works in their own home and looks after other people's children, sometimes alongside their own. They are professionals who provide **holistic care** and educational learning experiences. They will look after children of different ages, and need to plan for and resource play provision for them, as well as food and drink, rest and sleep, and nappy changing and toileting routines.
Teaching assistant	A teaching assistant works in a school, so in an early years environment will work in reception and nursery classes. They support the learning and development of young children between the ages of three and five years in these classes, and work on activities with individuals and groups. Teaching assistants also work with older children within the school, in a range of roles.
Nanny	A nanny usually works in the child's own home. They might live with the family or travel to the home each day. Nannies are employed to meet the needs of the children in the family within the home.

Activity

Go to the Early Years Alliance website to find out more about the role of an early years manager:

www.eyalliance.org.uk/what-makes-great-early-years-manager

What qualities does it say are needed?

Jargon buster

Holistic care: overall care of the child, valuing each area as important and interconnected. In this context, viewing the child as a whole person.

All staff within the setting have their own responsibilities which are part of their role, but they will all have the responsibilities shown in Figure 7.1.

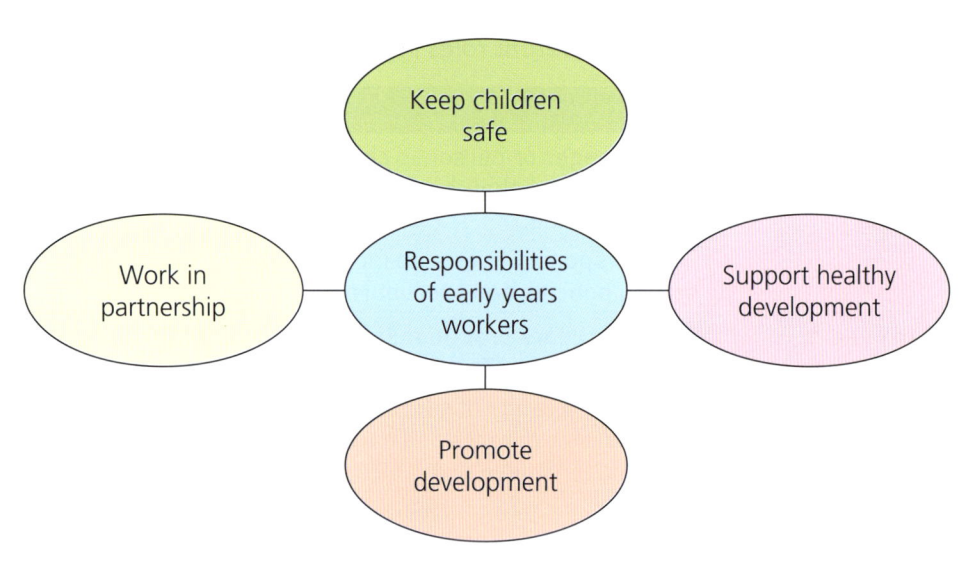

NCFE CACHE Level 1/2 Technical Award in Child Development and Care

Figure 7.1 Responsibilities of all staff in early years settings

Keep children safe

Table 7.2 outlines the main responsibilities of staff in keeping children safe. See Unit 5, section 5.2.3 for more information.

Table 7.2 Staff responsibilities for safety

Responsibility	What does this involve?
Prepare and maintain a safe environment	This includes checking that different areas of the setting are safe at all times.
Complete risk assessments	Risk assessments need to be done when carrying out new activities such as going out of the setting. (For more on risk assessments, see Unit 5, section 5.2.3.)
Work in partnership with others	All early years professionals need to be able to work as part of a team to make sure that babies and children are kept safe and well.
Provide supervision of children	Staff must supervise children to make sure that they are kept safe. All staff should understand the reasons why they need to manage safety. It is also important for the correct staff–child ratios to be followed when supervising children of different ages. This is set out in the EYFS statutory guidance.
Follow policy	Everyone in the setting should know about the setting's policies in each area to make sure that they are working **consistently** on safety issues. Any policy changes should be part of the whole staff's continuing professional development (CPD).

Check what you know

Name two aspects of an EYP's role.

Jargon buster

Consistently: for settings, this means everyone working to an agreed set of ideas.

138

7 Roles and responsibilities within early years settings

Support healthy development

It is the staff's responsibility to support children's healthy development through the following duties.

Provide access to healthy snacks, including fresh drinking water at mealtimes

To ensure that children understand the need for healthy snacks and meals, staff should make sure that they talk to children about why they are important.

The setting will have routines for snacks and mealtimes, which all staff should be familiar with. They also need to make sure that children have access to fresh drinking water when it is needed.

Support children's wellbeing

Children's wellbeing is an important aspect of their development, and as they develop relationships with children, key staff should enable them to talk about their feelings and emotions, particularly if they are upset, having a difficult time or their behaviour is affected. This will make staff members more approachable and encourage children to discuss anything they are worried about. It is likely to be part of the role of the Early Years SENDCo (special educational needs and disabilities co-ordinator) to support children and staff in how to approach this.

All settings also need to have a **DSL** so that staff can discuss any concerns about a child.

> **Jargon buster**
>
> **DSL:** designated safeguarding lead – the person in the setting who is responsible for monitoring and acting on safeguarding concerns.

Create opportunities for exercise

As well as having a well-equipped outdoor area, staff should give children opportunities to exercise while they are in the setting, and talk to them about why it is important.

Plan and support transitions

Staff should be able to plan and support expected transitions, such as moving house or changing settings, so that children are able to know about and understand what is happening. This is also important for transitions which are unexpected, such as bereavement. (For more on transitions, see Unit 2, section 2.4.)

Implement hygiene and health routines

Procedures such as hand washing after toileting and nappy changing should be part of the daily routine in the setting. Keeping kitchens and communal areas clean and talking to children about why this is important will also help them to understand how and why to keep healthy. (For more on hygiene and health routines, see Unit 3, section 3.2.1.)

Figure 7.2 Why is it important for staff to talk to children about the need for healthy meals and keeping communal areas clean?

Promote development

Early years practitioners are responsible for promoting children's development in the setting. To achieve this, they will need to follow these steps.

Plan development opportunities and activities

All staff need to show that they promote babies' and children's development in line with the EYFS. Practitioners should make sure that their plans cover all areas of learning and development through a range of learning programmes and activities. (For more on planning play activities and how they support children's development, see Unit 3, section 3.2.2 and Unit 9.)

> **Activity**
>
> Using the most recent version of the EYFS, look at the areas of learning and development.
> - What are the three prime areas and the four specific areas of learning and development?
> - Why are the prime areas important and how do they differ from the specific areas?

Talk to children during play, activities and routines

Talking is important. By providing a commentary or talking about what is happening, practitioners can help children with their communication and

7 Roles and responsibilities within early years settings

language development, as well as developing their general **cognitive skills**. In the early years, talking to children and helping to develop their ideas is often called **sustained shared thinking**.

Offer ideas and encouragement
Talking to the child, providing ideas and encouraging them during activities will support their emotional development, particularly if they are finding an activity challenging.

Create an enabling environment
The learning environment, both indoors and outdoors, needs to be stimulating and inclusive for all children. There should be plenty for them to look at and explore.

Observe and assess children's learning
All staff will be observing children as they carry out activities because this helps them to assess the children's learning. Early years staff will also be asked to carry out more structured observations and assessments, to make sure they know exactly what stage individual children are at in their learning and development. (For more on observations and assessments, see Unit 8.)

Plan activities and routines based on children's needs
If children have specific needs, practitioners should plan activities and routines to make sure that these can be met. For example, if a child has sensory needs such as a hearing impairment, it is important to make sure that they are able to take part in all the activities which are offered by the setting.

Adapt activities, resources and the environment
Practitioners might need to adapt activities or resources so that individual babies and children are able to use them. This means changing them slightly, for example bringing an activity down to the level of the child or changing the resources to help them to understand the activity, to ensure that it is inclusive.

> **Jargon buster**
>
> **Cognitive skills:** relating to the development of thinking and remembering.
>
> **Sustained shared thinking:** an activity in which two people, usually an adult and child, work together to solve a problem.

> **Theory into practice**
>
> Jamie is watching a group of three-year-old children who are playing in the water tray. They have containers, and are pouring and filling them.
> 1. How can Jamie support the children's learning while he is watching them?
> 2. How might he need to adapt the activity for a child who is visually impaired?

Work in partnership

Working in partnership is an important part of early years practitioners' responsibilities.

With parents/carers

All early years practitioners need to be able to work in partnership with parents and carers so that they can:

- get to know the children in their care better
- meet their needs more effectively.

This means communicating effectively with them and closely involving them in the activities of the setting.

With external professionals

External professionals are people who come into the setting to help support the needs of babies and children. Examples of external professionals are:

- speech and language therapists
- health professionals
- social workers
- family support workers.

(For more on these roles, see Unit 7, section 7.4.)

Participate in teamwork

Staff in early years settings need to work as part of a team with their colleagues. This means having good relationships and communicating effectively, so that children's needs can be met and any issues can be avoided.

(For more on partnership working, see Unit 7, section 7.2.1.)

> **Exam-style question**
>
> 1 Which of these is *not* the responsibility of everyone who works in an early years setting?
>   a Keeping children safe
>   b Promoting children's healthy development
>   c Working in partnership with others
>   d Referring children to specialists if they need additional support

7.2 Partnership working in the early years

Five things to know ...

1. Partnership working will be part of your role.
2. The partnerships may be within or outside the setting.
3. The partnership might be with an individual or with services.
4. Working in partnership helps everyone to support children and their families.
5. Effective partnerships depend on good communication and information sharing.

As we have seen, all early years practitioners need to work with other professionals so that they can meet the needs of the children and young people in their care. This will benefit not just the child and their parents but also the early years practitioner, through communicating effectively and sharing information.

7.2.1 How partnership working benefits the child, family and early years practitioner

Five things to know ...

1. Partnership working is an important aspect of early years practice.
2. Partnership working benefits parents, families and early years professionals as well as the child.
3. Working in partnership means that important information is shared between professionals sooner.
4. Partnership working creates shared goals between all those caring for a child.
5. Working in partnership puts families in touch with those who can provide support.

Jargon buster

Partnership working: different services and professionals working together with other teams or people to meet the child's and/or family's needs.

Partnership working and effective communication between different professionals is an important part of a practitioner's work with children, and this will have benefits in different areas. It will most importantly support the child but should also have advantages for families and early years practitioners.

Partnership working is particularly helpful where babies and young children have SEND, as there may be a range of professionals working with them.

Benefits to the child

Figure 7.3 highlights the different benefits to children of professionals working in partnership. These points are explained below.

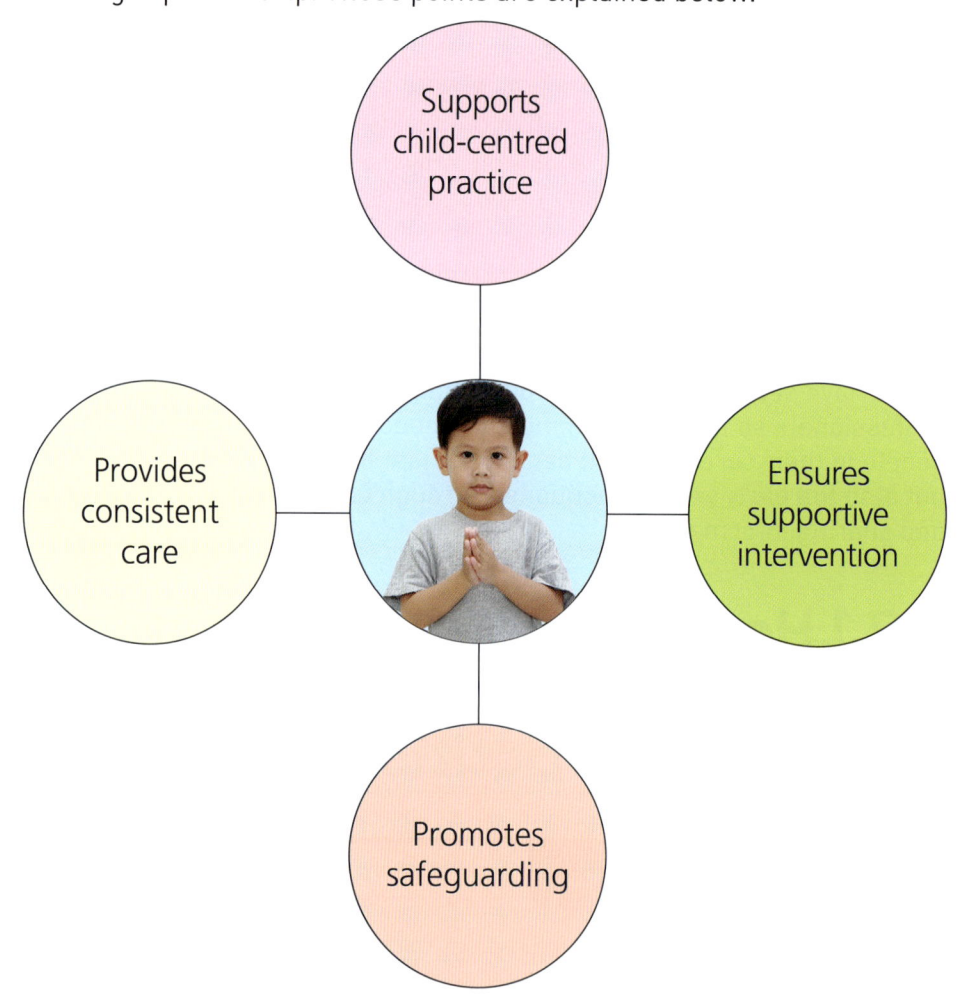

Figure 7.3 What are the benefits to the child of working in partnership?

Supports child-centred practice that meets children's holistic needs

When professionals work together, it means that the child and their needs are at the centre of their work. For example, if a parent has concerns about their child and passes these on to the early years practitioner, the concerns can also be discussed with specialists in the setting and beyond if necessary.

Ensures supportive intervention is made when a child is not meeting age-expected milestones

Sharing information means that practitioners and any other professionals who work with a child are made aware when that child is not at the expected stage of development for their age. This means that support and intervention to help the child can be put in place quickly.

Promotes safeguarding to ensure that children are protected from harm

Any safeguarding concerns need to be shared with the DSL straight away, so that they can be referred to others outside the setting. This will mean that the child is protected as soon as possible. (For more on safeguarding and the role of the DSL, see Unit 5, section 5.2.5 and also section 7.3.)

Provides consistent care, giving emotional and physical security

Young children should have routines and consistency so that they know what will happen next. Partnership working means that the child is supported consistently and understands that they will be cared for all the time, even if this is by different people. This will help them to feel reassured, and develop their confidence both physically and emotionally.

Benefits to the family

Gains support from practitioners with a different perspective or experience

The family will talk to different early years practitioners who might have different experiences or ideas. This may help families to develop new ways of relating to their child, and practitioners can also put them in touch with others who can support them.

> **Theory into practice**
>
> Benesh, who is from Afghanistan, is working in a setting. She has gained her early years qualification and is working as a room leader. Benesh hears a new parent who has come to the setting speaking Farsi, which she also speaks, and tells her manager that if they need support or translation services, she will be able to help. The manager suggests that Benesh comes to say hello to the parents and has an informal chat at pick-up time.
>
> 1 How will Benesh's actions support the child's family?
> 2 What other benefits might there be?

Ensures shared goals can be achieved and everyone is united in approach

It is important for all those working with a child to have shared goals and the same outlook. This means that they will all be able to work together to support the child and their family.

Builds trust so that information can be shared to support the child

Working with a range of professionals on a regular basis will mean that trust builds up between the family and the setting. A relationship will develop and the family will be more likely to share information to support the child.

Benefits to the early years practitioner

Access to advice and information which will inform planning of activities and routines to promote children's development

Partnership working makes it more straightforward for the early years practitioner to find information and advice from others. This in turn will help to promote children's development through planning individual activities and routines.

Builds trust and creates a supportive relationship where information can be shared

The more that professionals communicate with one another, the more trust will be built up between them as they will have developed a relationship. This means that they are more likely to share information regularly.

Supports shared goals, and everyone can work to their strengths and support each other

Having regular contact will also mean that professionals develop shared goals to support the children in their care. Everyone will be clear about what they need to do, which will help them to meet their objectives.

> **Activity**
>
> Create a poster for the meeting room at your setting, showing how partnership working supports and benefits everyone.

> **Exam-style questions**
>
> 2 Paul is working in an early years setting as a key person for Jess, who has cerebral palsy. She is supported by a number of health professionals as well as the other early years staff. The setting has a scheduled meeting every term with Jess' parents to discuss her progress and to enable all those working with her to share information.
>   a How will this routine support Jess and her family?
>   b What other benefits are there to working in this way?

7 Roles and responsibilities within early years settings

7.3 Specialist roles within early years settings

Five things to know ...

1. Some adults in the setting have additional responsibilities.
2. They will have knowledge and experience in different areas.
3. Some of these roles require extra qualifications.
4. All staff in the setting need to know who these specialists are.
5. All staff should know how to find and contact them when necessary.

There are a number of specialist roles in early years settings, shown in Table 7.3. People in these roles will have extra responsibilities to those listed in Table 7.1. In the case of childminders, these roles will all be part of their overall responsibilities, unless they have additional staff working with them.

Table 7.3 Specialist roles in early years settings

Specialist role	Responsibilities
Special educational needs and disabilities co-ordinator (SENDCo)	The SENDCo looks after and co-ordinates the provision within the setting for children who have SEND. They work closely with other staff within the setting and refer any concerns to specialists. The SENDCo is also responsible for overseeing, assessing, planning and monitoring the progress of these children. This role now requires an additional qualification in special needs education.
Designated safeguarding lead (DSL)	The DSL is the named person in the setting who is responsible for child protection. Staff should go to this person if they have any safeguarding concerns. The DSL makes sure that policies and procedures are in place to support safeguarding and makes referrals where they are needed. They also monitor the needs of children and their families and carers.
Physical activity and nutrition co-ordinator (PANCo)	The PANCo is the person in the setting who is responsible for promoting health and wellbeing. They act as a champion for best practice in physical activity and nutrition, and are the leaders for managing positive change around health. The PANCo will support and advise parents and carers, as well as liaising with other staff. They will need to have an additional qualification to do this.
Key person	A key person for each child is a requirement of the EYFS. Each key person will be responsible for a group of children and will get to know them and their families. They will develop relationships with them so that they and the setting can work together to meet the best interests of the child and help to support their growth and development.

Check what you know

Name three of the responsibilities of a SENDCo.

NCFE CACHE Level 1/2 Technical Award in Child Development and Care

> **Exam-style question**
>
> 3 You have been asked to go to a meeting about a child who will be starting at the setting, as you will be the child's key person. The child has some health conditions and developmental issues which they need support with. Which of the specialists in Table 7.3 might also be attending the meeting, and why?

7.4 Specialist roles outside early years settings

> **Five things to know …**
>
> 1. Specialists sometimes come from outside the setting to help and advise families and staff.
> 2. They provide support for specific issues.
> 3. All staff should know how to contact specialists when needed. This may be through the SENDCo or DSL.
> 4. External specialists are professionals who are trained in health care, social care or special educational needs.
> 5. Specialists may be needed on a one-off basis or throughout a child's time at the setting.

Sometimes, you will meet different professionals who come into the early years setting to support and advise parents/carers and staff about the needs of a child. These specialist roles have professional knowledge and experience about the areas of SEND, health or social care.

SEND teams

These teams work with children who have SEND and their families. As there are a number of different areas of special educational need, SEND teams may be made up of different professionals. For your qualification, you need to know about the work of physiotherapists and educational psychologists.

Physiotherapist

A physiotherapist helps an individual affected by injury, disability or illness with movement and exercise, manual therapy, education and advice. In early years settings, they are most likely to be working with children who need help with physical mobility. This means that the child has physical needs, and needs help and support to move. This may be their fine or gross motor skills, or in both areas.

7 Roles and responsibilities within early years settings

> **Theory into practice**
>
> Lola has a condition called scoliosis, which means that the bones in her spine have not formed properly and cause it to be curved. She wears a back brace to stop it from getting worse.
>
> Lola has regular visits to the physiotherapist, who is coming into the setting today with Lola's mum to give the staff some advice about the therapy she is receiving and how to support her needs.
>
> 1 Why is it important for the physiotherapist to support and advise the staff in the setting as well as Lola's parents?
> 2 How else will the setting benefit from having contact with Lola's physiotherapist?

Educational psychologist

An educational psychologist might be asked to come into the setting to assess a child who has SEND, including emotional or behavioural difficulties. They will be able to give advice on how the setting can manage a child's learning and behaviour, and what might be the next steps. They are likely to be involved if a child already has or if the setting is applying for an **Education, Health and Care Plan (EHCP)** for additional funding to support them in the setting and beyond.

> **Jargon buster**
>
> **Education, Health and Care Plan (EHCP):** a document which outlines the support a child or young person needs to meet their potential while they are in the education system and up to the age of 25.

If you are supporting a child who has SEND, you might also meet occupational therapists, speech and language therapists, specialists in sensory support or others, depending on the needs of the child. Remember that not all SEND will be visible to others.

Figure 7.4 You might meet children with a range of SEND who benefit from sensory experiences where directed by specialists

Health professionals

Health professionals work with babies, children and their families within the community. They are likely to be the first professionals to work with the child, and as a result they are in a good position to identify any health or developmental needs in the child as early as possible.

Table 7.4 Health care professionals who work with settings

Health professional's title	What is their role?
GP	A GP diagnoses and treats medical conditions. They might refer a baby or child to other professionals if they have concerns about their development, and be involved in writing reports or giving advice to parents.
Paediatrician	This is a doctor who specialises in the treatment and care of babies, children and young people. They have additional training and experience, and work with a range of professionals to support children and their families, particularly if they have long-term medical conditions.
Health visitor	This is a nurse or midwife who has had additional training. They will work with children from birth to five years and their families to support and promote health and development. Their role varies from support at the start of parenthood to giving advice on childhood accidents.

Activity

Research the roles of the health visitor and paediatrician, and record what you have found out.

Read and write

Make a list of the different external professionals who might come into the setting. Give a brief description of what they do.

Children's social care

You might come into contact with two specialists regarding children's social care: a social worker and a family support worker.

Social worker

The role of a social worker is to:

- assess the needs of a child and their family
- offer support to ensure a child is protected and well cared for.

Social workers work with children and their families who have problems or are at risk, and visit their clients in different settings. They refer clients to other agencies to gain the support they need.

As well as working with children and families, social workers also work with elderly people, homeless families, young offenders and people with learning and physical disabilities.

Family support worker

A family support worker provides practical advice and support to individuals and families in need on a range of issues.

7 Roles and responsibilities within early years settings

These issues may include:

- debt, drug and alcohol addiction
- parenting skills
- bereavement.

They will be asked to work with a family by social services, and will build a close relationship with the family and help them to work through their challenges. Their role depends on the needs of the family, and they might specialise in a particular area. In some cases, their work helps to ensure that a child stays with their family.

Extend

Consider the benefits of a range of internal and external professionals who might come into the setting. How do they support children and their families?

Check what you know

What do you know about the role of a social worker?

Test yourself

1. Name **three** different roles which may be found within an early years setting.
2. What is the role of a nanny?
3. Where does a childminder usually work?
4. How does an early years practitioner support the child's healthy development?
5. Name **two** other professionals who an early years practitioner might work in partnership with as part of their role.
6. Outline how partnership working benefits the child.
7. Why are there some specialist roles within an early years setting?
8. Describe the role of the SENDCo.
9. How does a health visitor support young children and their families?
10. Name **one** external professional who might be on a team supporting a baby or child who has SEND, and explain their role.

Assignment practice

Case study

You are the key person for Theo, aged four, who has a diagnosis of acute lymphoblastic leukaemia. This is a type of childhood cancer, and makes Theo very tired. Additional symptoms are that he is reluctant to eat and has pain in his joints, which makes it difficult to take part in some activities. You are spending more time with him than your other key children as he understandably needs emotional as well as physical support.

The setting is working towards having an EHCP for Theo. He will need to be assessed, and the setting has asked for a meeting with all the professionals who work with him, as well as his parents, so that they can talk about how they will do this and gather as much information together as possible.

Task

1. Identify the different professionals who might be involved in supporting Theo and who may be asked to the meeting.
2. Discuss the importance of additional support for Theo in the setting and why an EHCP would be beneficial for him.
3. Give examples of some activities to support Theo which might be possible with additional help.

8 The importance of observations in early years childcare

About this content area

All settings which work with children need to know how they are developing. Practitioners do this by watching and listening as children play and take part in activities. This process is known as 'observations'. In this unit, we look at the importance of observations, how they may be carried out and also how to share them with others.

8.1 Observation and recording methods
- 8.1.1 How observations support child development
- 8.1.2 Objective and subjective observation
- 8.1.3 Components of recording observations
- 8.1.4 Different methods of observation
- 8.1.5 Sharing observations

8.1 Observation and recording methods

Five things to know ...

1. Observations are used in all early years settings.
2. Observations are about gaining information about children.
3. Information gained from observations is used for assessment.
4. Ongoing assessments are called formative.
5. Summative assessments look at children's progress over a period of time.

All adults working with children in early years settings will learn how to observe and record information about children's progress, and also their interests. There are many different ways of observing and recording information about children. We look at these later on in this unit. The information from observations is used to assess different things, including whether a child needs more help.

There are two types of assessment: formative and summative.

1. Formative assessment is where information is used to make decisions about what a child needs and how best to work with them in an ongoing way.
2. Summative assessment is where information is used to 'sum up' how a child is doing over a period of time.

We look more at formative and summative assessments in the next section.

8 The importance of observations in early years childcare

8.1.1 How observations support child development

> **Five things to know ...**
> 1. Observations provide information for assessments.
> 2. There are two types of assessment: formative and summative.
> 3. Formative assessments are important for short-term planning.
> 4. Summative assessments are important for long-term planning.
> 5. Information from assessments can be shared with parents/carers and professionals.

The term 'observations' is used to describe the process of noticing how children are developing. While adults routinely observe children, there will be moments when observations need to be recorded. (See section 8.1.4 for recording methods.)

Observations that are recorded are used to assess children. We have seen already that there are two types of assessment: formative and summative.

> **Check what you know**
>
> What is the difference between formative and summative assessment?

How formative assessment is used

Formative assessment is used for many different purposes:

- To plan and respond to children
  Formative assessment is used so that adults can respond immediately to children's developmental needs. They may do this by planning activities, putting out resources and creating a rich environment. Adults may also think about their role in following children's interests and supporting their development.
- To find out the child's interests
  By watching children as they play, share books and use other resources, adults can work out what the child is interested in. This information is used to help planning.
- To help identify stages of development
  By observing children, adults look to see how children are developing. They may notice that a baby is sitting unsupported and so organise resources differently to allow the baby to reach out for them. In the same way, an adult may notice that a three-year-old's sense of balance is developing well. They may look for more challenging activities involving balance, such as a wobble board.

Figure 8.1 What can you observe about this two-year-old's development?

- To understand triggers in behaviour
  Formative assessment can help practitioners to work out why children are showing certain behaviours, and how best to help the child.
- To gain insight to share with parent/carer/professionals
  Working with parents, carers and other professionals is important. Formative assessment is used to share information with them. (See Unit 7 for the benefits of working in partnership with parents, carers and other professionals.)
- To support provision for the characteristics of effective teaching and learning
  As part of the EYFS, practitioners need to think about how individual children learn best, and then use this information to plan. By observing children's responses to different situations, practitioners can think about how best to motivate, engage and develop children's problem solving.
- To plan development activities
  Through formative assessment, practitioners can work out what a child's next steps will be in different aspects of their development. A child who can snip dough using scissors might be ready to snip pieces of paper, or even cut a piece of paper in half.

Theory into practice

Priti is three years old. She started at the nursery this week. Her key person is observing her closely. The key person notes that Priti spends a lot of time in the book area and also in the home corner where she plays with other children. Yesterday, the key person noticed that Priti wanted to join in a sponge painting activity, but was worried about

8 The importance of observations in early years childcare

her hands touching the paint. Today, the key person notices that Priti stops playing in the sand to wash her hands.
1 What information has the key person learnt about Priti so far?
2 How might this information help the key person work with Priti?
3 What information might the key person discuss with parents/carers to find out more about meeting Priti's needs?

Summative assessment

Summative assessments 'sum up' what children know and can do at a point in time. An example of a summative assessment is the two-year-old progress check. When children turn two, early years settings write a report that looks at the child's development (see page 71).

Summative assessments are also used for many different reasons:

- **To evaluate the effectiveness of interventions**
  Some children need extra help or support. This is called an intervention. A summative assessment might look at how well the strategies or resources are working.
- **To support assessment of the child's development**
  It is important to check that children's development is typical. Where a child is showing delay, it might mean that they need extra help. A summative assessment will compare a child's progress to the expected development of children of that age.
- **To support other professionals**
  Some children and families are helped by other professionals. This might be a speech and language therapist or a social worker. Early years settings share summative assessments so that other professionals can see how a child is progressing. Early years settings have to ask parents/carers for permission to do this.
- **To plan learning and development activities**
  The information from a summative assessment helps early years settings to work out what activities and resources a child needs next. For example, a child who is walking well might enjoy pushing a pram or wheelbarrow. In some cases, it may be that a child will need additional support and time from an adult in the setting. In other cases, a child may need more specialist care or resources.
- **To track progress against current framework requirements**
  Early years settings follow the EYFS (see page 70). It has seven areas of learning and development. For each area of learning and development, there are goals. Early years settings will look at how children are making progress towards these goals.

> **Jargon buster**
>
> **Intervention:** resources or support to help a child with their learning or development

NCFE CACHE Level 1/2 Technical Award in Child Development and Care

Activity

Flynn is 12 months old. His childminder has completed a summative assessment. She notes that he can crawl, sit and reach for toys. He also pulls himself up to standing. He can point to pictures in books and makes marks on paper.

- Using the information from Unit 1, identify whether Flynn's development is typical for his age.
- Explain why a summative assessment is used to assess development.
- Name two resources that the childminder can use to promote Flynn's development.

Check what you know

Explain the reasons why a summative assessment might be used.

Extend

Early years settings that take two-year-old children will carry out a summative assessment. It is called the two-year-old progress check.

- Download a copy of the statutory framework for the EYFS.
- Read about the information which has to be collected in this assessment.
- What is the purpose of this check, and why is it an example of a summative assessment?

Exam-style question

1. Why might settings carry out formative as well as summative assessments?

8.1.2 Objective and subjective observation

Five things to know ...

1. Observations can be objective or subjective.
2. Objective observations record only what is said or has happened, without any judgement or opinions.
3. Objective observations are more accurate.
4. Subjective observations are influenced by the observer's own views.
5. Subjective observations are less accurate.

Jargon buster

Subjective observation: the observation is based on opinions and personal views.

The way practitioners observe children can make a difference to the information that they get. It is possible for two people to observe the same child at the same time and write two very different observations. This is because one might be a **subjective observation** where the person

8 The importance of observations in early years childcare

has written down what they think, rather than what they see and hear, which is an **objective observation**.

Objective observations

One of the skills in observing and assessing children is to be objective. Figure 8.2 shows the features of an objective assessment.

> **Jargon buster**
>
> **Objective observation:** the observation is based on facts.

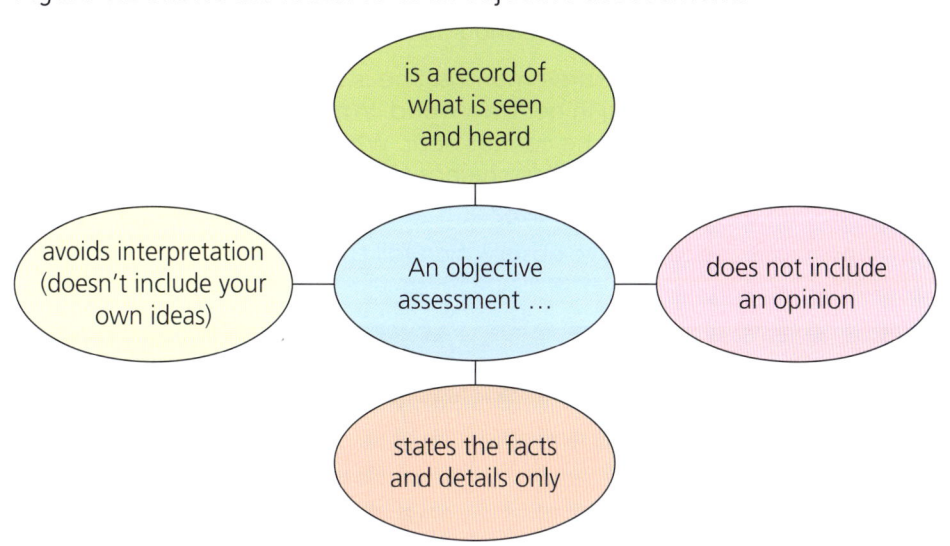

An objective assessment …
- is a record of what is seen and heard
- avoids interpretation (doesn't include your own ideas)
- does not include an opinion
- states the facts and details only

Figure 8.2 Features of an objective assessment

Being objective is important, as the information that is recorded is more likely to be accurate.

> **Check what you know**
>
> Can you explain why it is important that observations are objective?

Subjective observations

Subjective observations are not useful as the observer has already made up their mind about what a child knows and can do. Figure 8.3 shows the features of a subjective observation.

Subjective observation is …
- influenced by past events
- subject to interpretation
- based on personal experience
- based on opinion, feelings or assumption

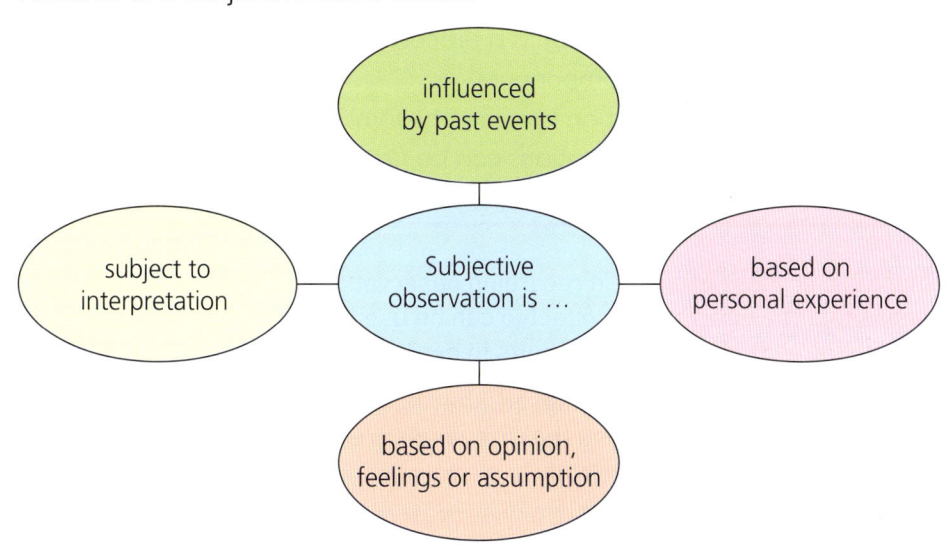

Figure 8.3 Features of a subjective observation

If an observer is doing a subjective observation, they might miss something that is important because they have already made up their minds.

> **Check what you know**
>
> Write down three features of a subjective observation.

157

NCFE CACHE Level 1/2 Technical Award in Child Development and Care

Theory into practice

Here are two observations. One is objective and the other is subjective:

Martha is four years and three months. Martha is sitting at the table doing a jigsaw. She is alone. The adult is calling her name. She does not respond. She carries on putting the pieces of jigsaw puzzle together. The adult taps her gently on the shoulder. Martha looks up and smiles.

Martha is four years and three months. She is sitting doing a jigsaw all by herself. She likes being in her own world. When the adult calls her name, she pretends that she cannot hear. When the adult taps her on the shoulder, she is pleased that she has the attention.

1. Which observation is objective?
2. Why might the subjective observation fail to pick up a hearing loss?

Exam-style question

2. Which of these describes an objective observation?
   - a Influenced by past events
   - b Based on personal experience
   - c Based on opinion
   - d A record of what is seen or heard

8.1.3 Components of recording observations

Five things to know ...

1. Carrying out an observation is a process.
2. There are four main components.
3. Assessing the information from an observation is important.
4. Information from observations can be used for planning.
5. The quality of an observation affects how it is evaluated.

There is a process involved in recording observations. Following the process means that the information collected can be used to support the child. It often takes a lot of practice for adults to become good at observing children.

Before adults can observe children, they have to have permission from parents and carers. They must also make sure that the information from observations is kept confidential.

There are four different stages in completing an observation, shown in Figure 8.4.

8 The importance of observations in early years childcare

1 Aim
This is the information that the observer wants to find out about the child, such as how well a child is talking or walking up steps. Having a clear aim helps the observer to be detailed in their observation.

2 Recording
This is the actual observation. An observer may film a child or simply watch them and make notes.

3 Evaluation
This is an assessment or conclusion about what has been observed and recorded. When evaluating, practitioners think about what they have learnt by observing the child. They might use reference books to help them work out if what they have seen is typical for the age.

4 Planning
The last step is to think about how to support the child's development further. This might include using different resources or activities, or changing the way that the adult works with the child.

Figure 8.4 The four stages of an observation

Check what you know
Write down the four components of an observation.

8.1.4 Different methods of observation

Five things to know …

1. There are many different methods of recording observations.
2. There are advantages and disadvantages to each method.
3. Most early years settings use more than one method.
4. The reason why a child is being observed will affect the choice of method.
5. It takes time to learn each observation method.

Early years settings use a variety of methods to observe and record children's development. We have seen that observations are used to help plan activities and also to identify whether a child needs more help. When observations are recorded, the information gained about a child is confidential.

In this section we will look at five approaches to recording observations.

Activity
Visit an early years setting or talk to a member of staff. What methods do they use to record children's development?

Media methods

Over recent years, more settings are using technology to help record children's development. Recordings are made in digital format which can be copied or shared securely online with children's parents/carers.

There are several things for settings to think about when using media methods:

- Settings have to get parents'/carers' permission to use digital media.
- Settings have to keep digital records secure.

There are two main ways that early years settings use media methods: video/film and photographs.

Making a video/film recording

It is possible to film a child or children by using a variety of devices, including a tablet, digital camera or mobile phone. To avoid breaking confidentiality, most settings have a device that is only used in the setting for this purpose.

Table 8.1 Benefits and disadvantages of making a video/film recording

Benefits	Disadvantages
Can be played back to see what a child is doing	Can be difficult to hear what a child is saying in a noisy room
Easy to do	Children might start to act differently when they see a camera
Can be put online for parents/carers to see	

Taking a photograph

A photograph shows a snapshot of what a child is doing or what they have made. Photos can be printed out for parents/carers or used as part of a display in the setting.

Table 8.2 Benefits and disadvantages of taking a photo

Benefits	Disadvantages
Easy to do	Does not provide information about why, how and what the child is doing
Can be put online for parents/carers to see	
Good for recording something that has been made, e.g. a model made of blocks	Children may start to pose if they see a camera

Learning journal

Learning journals are popular in early years settings. The idea is that a range of different observations are put into a book which can be shared with parents and the child.

Observations might include photographs, notes and thoughts about the child's development. Children's progress and also their interests can be seen over time.

8 The importance of observations in early years childcare

Some learning journals are now put online so that parents/carers can look at them from home.

Table 8.3 Benefits and disadvantages of a learning journal

Benefits	Disadvantage
Provides a record of a child's time in a setting	Can be time-consuming to create
Can encourage parents/carers to take an interest in their child's development	

Sticky notes

The idea behind using sticky notes (e.g. Post-it® notes) is to jot down something that the child has done that is significant. This might be a child's behaviour or a skill.

Once the note is completed, it can be put into a folder or displayed on a board for other team members or the child's parents to see.

Table 8.4 Benefits and disadvantages of using sticky notes

Benefits	Disadvantages
Very quick to do	May not provide enough detail to be useful
Easy to share with others	Notes may be lost if not filed quickly
Can be used as a starting point for longer observations	

Narrative observation

A narrative observation is when a child is observed for a short amount of time and the adult writes down everything that the child says and does. Narrative observations are also called 'free description' and 'written account'.

Table 8.5 Benefits and disadvantages of a narrative observation

Benefits	Disadvantage
Can provide a lot of information about a child's learning and development	Hard to write down everything that the child does in the time
Can help the adult to learn more about a child's interests and how they learn	

> **Activity**
>
> With permission of parents/carers/guardians, spend five minutes observing a child. Try and write down as much as you can.
> - How did you find this process?
> - What did you learn about this child's development?

Checklists

A checklist is a list of skills or knowledge that the adult is hoping to observe. When the adult sees the skill or knowledge that is on the list, they write a comment and/or put a tick. This is why the term 'tick chart' is also used. Most checklists are linked to developmental milestones.

161

There are two ways of carrying out a checklist:

1 The practitioner asks a child to do something that is on the checklist. For example, 'Can you find your name?'
2 The practitioner simply observes the child over a few days and ticks off the chart when they see the child naturally do something.

Table 8.6 Benefits and disadvantages of a checklist

Benefits	Disadvantages
Easy to use	If children are asked to do things, they might become anxious
Can help to spot if children are not showing expected progress	Does not record information about why children find a skill easy or difficult

> **Check what you know**
>
> Write down the four components of an observation.

> **Exam-style question**
>
> 3 Identify **one** advantage and **one** disadvantage of using the sticky note method to observe children.

8.1.5 Sharing observations

> **Five things to know ...**
>
> 1 Information from observations is usually shared.
> 2 Sharing observations helps to meet children's needs.
> 3 Sharing observations helps everyone to monitor a child's progress.
> 4 Sharing observations can help practitioners to organise early interventions.
> 5 Parents and carers have to give their permission before information is shared with other professionals.

The information from observations and assessments is usually shared with others. This helps the setting to find out more about how a child is doing and also how best to support them. You must gain permission from parents and carers before sharing information with other professionals.

Figure 8.5 shows who observations may be shared with.

8 The importance of observations in early years childcare

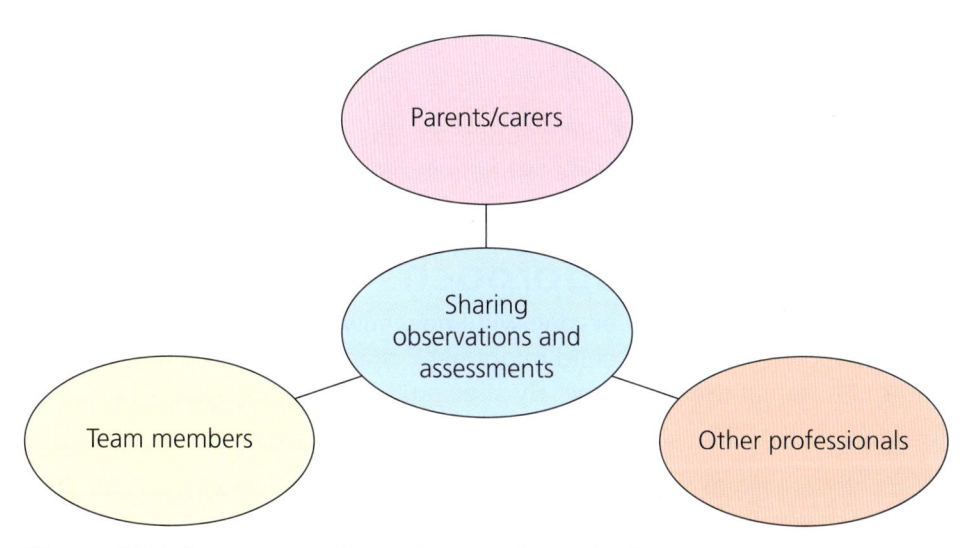

Figure 8.5 Who can you share observations with?

There are many reasons why observations and assessments are shared.

Continuity of care

Sharing information means that everyone can respond to the child in the same way. For example, as a result of observing a two-year-old child, it is agreed to move their nap time forward by an hour.

> **Activity**
>
> Josef is going to start the reception class in a few weeks' time. His parents are happy for the nursery to share information from observations with the reception teacher. Josef's key person shares information about how Josef gets worried when there are changes to the routine. He often cries or tries to run away. His key person explains the strategies the setting uses that seem to help Josef cope when there are changes to the routines.
> - Why is it important for the nursery to share information from observations with the reception teacher?
> - How can the reception teacher use this information to help Josef?
> - What other information about Josef's development might the reception teacher find helpful?

Monitoring progress

Everyone who spends time with a child will see different things. By sharing observations, parents/carers and other professionals can find out what skills and knowledge the child shows when they are in the early years setting.

Ideally, parents and other professionals will also share their observations. This helps everyone to monitor a child's progress.

Early intervention

When a child's development is not typical, they might need additional support or interventions. Sharing observations with parents/carers, team members and other professionals makes sure that children get this support.

Child-centred approach

By sharing information, everyone will know how best to meet an individual child's needs. A child might need more time to dress than other children of the same age. By sharing this information, adults can make sure that extra time is given.

Read and write

Create a leaflet that explains the importance of observing and assessing children. Your leaflet should include:
- the reasons why observation and assessment are important
- the four components of recording an observation
- an explanation of why it is important to be objective.

Test your knowledge

1. Explain the meaning of the term 'summative assessment'.
2. What is the difference between an objective and a subjective observation?
3. Why is it important to avoid carrying out a subjective observation?
4. Identify **three** components of an observation.
5. Why is it important for observations to have an aim?
6. What is meant by the term 'learning journal'?
7. Give **one** advantage and **one** disadvantage of using a checklist.
8. Explain what a narrative record is and why it might be used.
9. Give **three** reasons why it is important for adults to share observations.
10. Explain why sharing observations might support children's development.

Assignment practice

Case study
Katia's son is starting at a nursery. The staff have said that they will be carrying out regular observations, and have asked for her permission. Katia has asked you for information about observations and assessments, and how they are used in early years settings.

Task
1. Prepare an email that you can send to Katia with the following information:
   - the difference between summative and formative assessments
   - methods of observing children
   - how this information might be used
   - how observations and assessments are used in the setting.
2. Katia has also asked for your advice about whether she should give permission for the setting to pass on information to other professionals. As part of your answer, give a rationale for your advice.

9 Planning in early years childcare

About this content area

Planning is an important part of an early years practitioner's work. It helps them know what resources, experiences and activities to prepare and do with children, and to think about how best to help children develop and learn. Practitioners use the information from observations to help them with planning (see also Unit 8).

This unit explores the importance of planning and looks at ways in which early years settings might plan.

9.1 The purpose of a child-centred approach
9.2 The purpose of the planning cycle
9.3 The planning cycle

9.1 The purpose of a child-centred approach

Five things to know …

1. A child-centred approach means thinking about children's needs, wishes and interests.
2. Early years settings use a child-centred approach in the way that they work.
3. A child-centred approach to play allows children to direct their own play and gives children opportunities to make their own choices.
4. A child-centred approach gives children opportunities to explore, question and problem solve.
5. A child-centred approach means that adults are responsive to children's needs and stage of development.

In this section we look at the term 'child-centred' and explore what a child-centred approach to play means.

'Child-centred' is a term that is often used in early years. It means making children's needs, wishes and interests a priority. When early years settings use a child-centred approach, children are happier. Their development is also better as their needs are being met.

NCFE CACHE Level 1/2 Technical Award in Child Development and Care

> **Check what you know**
>
> What is meant by the term 'child-centred approach'?

There are many ways in which a child-centred approach is used in early years settings. These include:

- settling in at a child's pace
- letting a child choose which book to share.

Exam-style question

1. Which statement explains what a child-centred approach means?
   a. Children can do what they want.
   b. Adults observe children before acting.
   c. Children's needs and interests are focused on.
   d. Children play outdoors most of the time.

Extend

Reggio Emilia is an approach to early years that is known for being child-centred. Some nurseries have adopted this approach in the UK.

- Carry out some research using the internet to find out about the Reggio Emilia approach. You may find the following websites useful:

  www.reggiochildren.it/en/reggio-emilia-approach

  www.daynurseries.co.uk/advice/the-reggio-emilia-approach-to-early-years-education

- Write a short report outlining the Reggio Emilia approach and what this would mean for day-to-day practice in a nursery.

A child-centred approach to play

As part of the planning cycle, practitioners will plan for play because it is a way of meeting children's needs and interests. Most early years settings use a child-centred approach when they plan for play. This means:

- Children can choose what to do and how to play.
- Adults will be there to support children.

Children might want them to join the play. Sometimes children ask for help, or an adult might spot that they need more resources.

When a child-centred approach and planning is used, children concentrate and persevere. This is because they have chosen what to do. It also allows them to form relationships with other children.

9 Planning in early years childcare

9.2 The purpose of the planning cycle

Five things to know …

1. The planning cycle helps meet children's needs and interests.
2. It helps to identify children's needs and development.
3. It can be used to target activities to help children.
4. It can be used to help parents/carers and other professionals work together.
5. It can be used when referring a child to other professionals.

The needs and interests of babies and young children are constantly changing. To meet their needs, early years settings need to plan carefully. They do this using a planning cycle.

The planning cycle is divided into five stages, as shown in Figure 9.1. In the next section, we will look at each of the different stages.

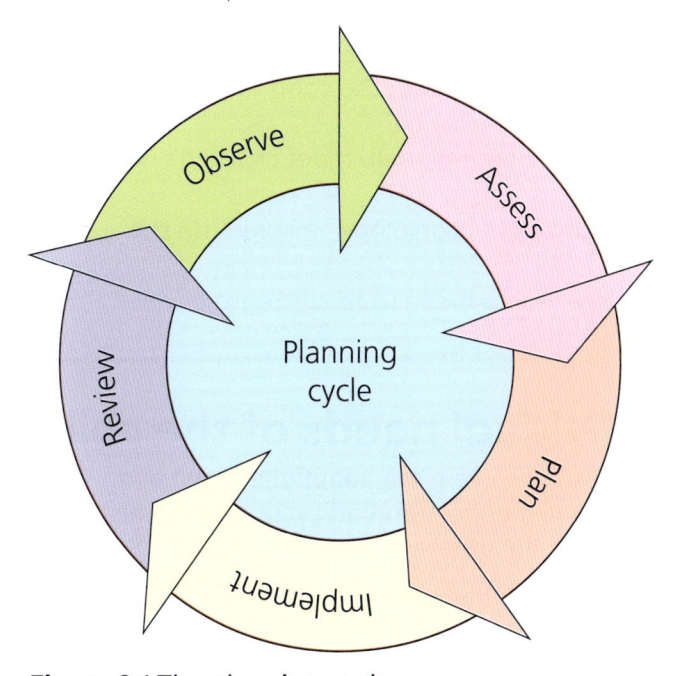

Figure 9.1 The planning cycle

In Unit 8 we looked at observation and assessment. Can you see that they are part of the planning cycle? There are several reasons why the planning cycle is important.

NCFE CACHE Level 1/2 Technical Award in Child Development and Care

Create a well-planned environment

The term 'environment' is used to describe everything that surrounds a child indoors and outdoors. A well-planned environment is one which meets children's needs to play and explore, talk and feel comfortable.

The planning cycle can be used to plan a stimulating and comfortable environment that will help children learn. One of the ways that children learn is by talking to adults and other children. A well-planned environment will encourage children and adults to interact. Some of this interaction may happen in the moment because children see something that is of interest to them.

> **Theory into practice**
>
> Staff at Little Blossoms Pre-school have a meeting each week to think about the toys, resources and activities that will be put out each day. As part of their planning, they think about what children have enjoyed using, but also what has not worked so well.
>
> Today, they are thinking about changing the furniture around to create some smaller spaces indoors. They have noticed that some children seem to talk more to adults in cosy spaces. They are also going to put out some new equipment with the sand to develop a few of the children's fine motor skills.
>
> 1. How might changing the environment help meet children's needs and interests?
> 2. Why is it important for adults to observe how children use the environment?
> 3. Explain how the planning cycle is being used to create a well-planned environment.

> **Check what you know**
>
> What are the two stages of the planning cycle that are important in identifying a child's needs?

Identify the individual needs of the child

The first two stages of the planning cycle are about observing and assessing. This means that by using the planning cycle, adults can think about children's development in the different areas.

Here are some practical examples of how the planning cycle works to identify the individual needs of the child.

9 Planning in early years childcare

Physical development
An adult might notice that a baby is pushing up on all fours. This means that the baby is nearly crawling. To encourage this, the adult then makes sure that the baby has more time playing on the floor.

Social and emotional development
The adult notices that a new child seems to enjoy playing in the home corner. They think that the child feels more secure in this small space. The adult creates some other small spaces so that the child can try out other activities.

Identifying the individual needs of children

Cognitive development
The adult watches a child complete a 12-piece jigsaw easily. The adult identifies that the child may need more problem-solving challenges. They start planning puzzle-type activities for the child.

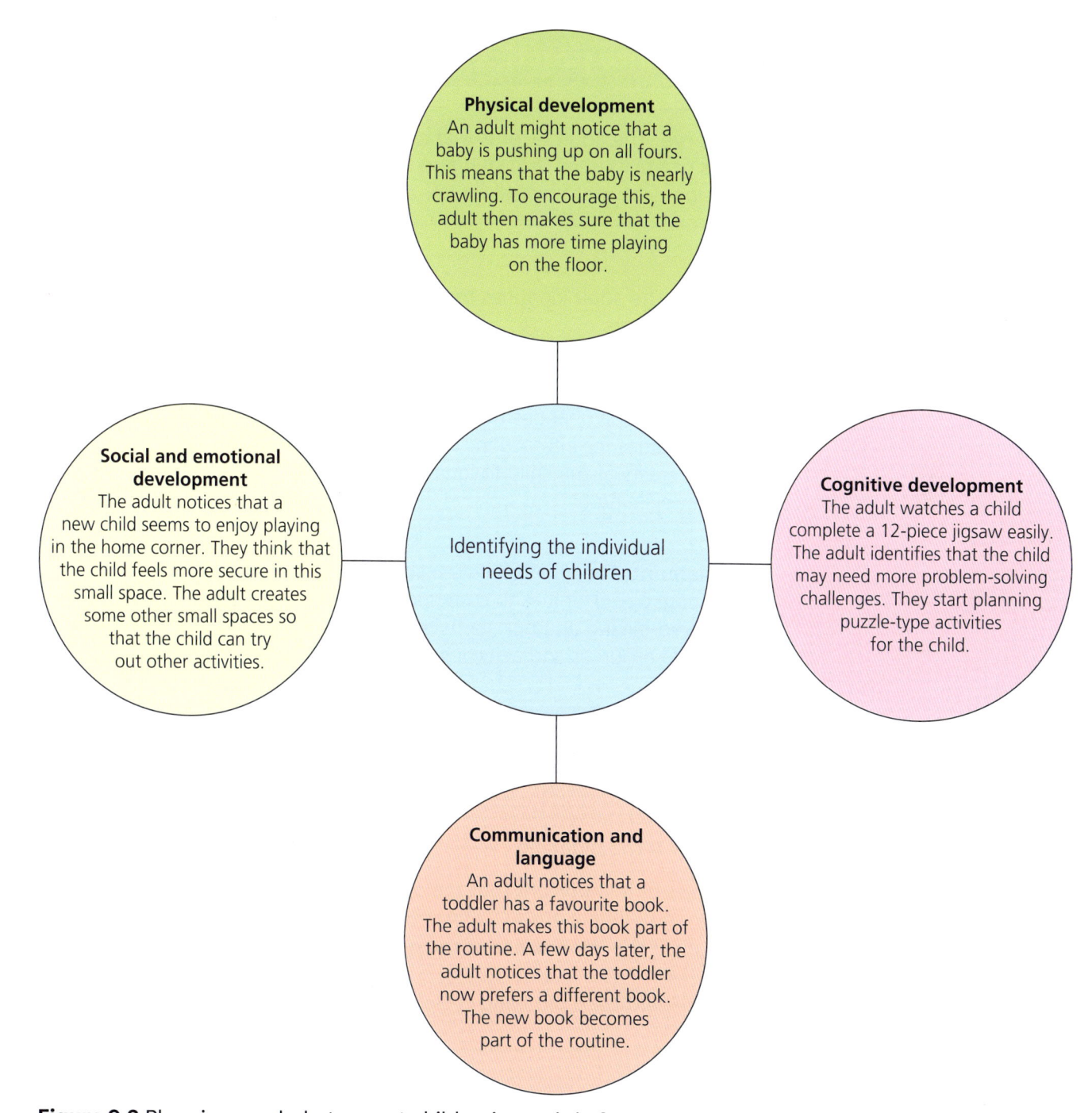

Communication and language
An adult notices that a toddler has a favourite book. The adult makes this book part of the routine. A few days later, the adult notices that the toddler now prefers a different book. The new book becomes part of the routine.

Figure 9.2 Planning can help to meet children's needs in four areas

Identify support needs

As children grow and develop, their needs and interests change. Sometimes information gained from observations (see Unit 8) will show that children need support with their learning and development. The planning cycle helps adults to think about how best to support these needs.

Theory into practice

Observe: The adult records that a three-year-old child is showing signs of frustration. The adult also notes that the child's language development is not typical for her age/stage.

↓

Assess: The adult identifies that the child needs more support with language.

↓

Plan: The adult changes the routine so that the child has more opportunities for interaction. The adult also plans around the needs and interests of the child to ignite and stimulate their interest in communicating.

↓

Implement: The adult uses their skills to make sure that the child has more opportunities to communicate in a variety of ways, including talking and non-verbal communication. The adult also chooses resources and activities that will encourage interaction.

↓

Review: The adult thinks about the resources and activities and how well they have worked. The adult also thinks about whether the strategy has increased how much time the child has spent talking.

Figure 9.3 The planning cycle in action

1. Why was it important that the adult observed and assessed the child before planning any activities or resources to encourage interaction?
2. Explain the importance of the adult reviewing how the plan has worked.
3. Consider how a planning cycle might assist a child who needs more support.

Activity

Create a poster that shows the five stages of the planning cycle.

Next to each stage, write a description of what is involved.

Establish action planning

The planning cycle can be used for action planning. If a child has many different needs, adults may decide on what to focus on. They can then review the child's progress and the child's responses.

Develop partnership working

Other adults such as parents or other professionals might help with planning. Their observations about a child might be used when planning activities, resources and play opportunities. By involving other people, children's needs are more likely to be met, as information is shared and also discussed.

Refer the child to other professionals

The planning cycle is sometimes used when referring children to other professionals. For example, a speech and language therapist might want to know what a nursery has already done to help a child. They might also want practitioners to think about how well the interventions are working. Practitioners can then feed back information which in turn could be used for the next cycle of planning.

> **Exam-style question**
>
> 2 Give an example of how the planning cycle might be used to refer a child to professionals.

> **Check what you know**
>
> Give two reasons why the planning cycle is important.

9.3 The planning cycle

> **Five things to know ...**
>
> 1 Planning is a cycle.
> 2 There are five stages in the planning cycle.
> 3 Each stage is important.
> 4 The first stage is to observe children.
> 5 After the final stage, adults start the cycle again.

Stages of the planning cycle

We have seen why the planning cycle is important. In this section we look at each of the stages of the planning cycle.

Observe

This part of the planning cycle is about observing a child's holistic or overall growth and development. Practitioners may watch how a child plays, talks or responds to different situations. See also Unit 8.

Assess

The assessment part of the cycle means thinking about what the observations mean for the child. To help with the assessment, adults will compare how a child is doing with the milestones for their age. We looked at this in Unit 1: milestones are the knowledge and skills that children show at different ages.

In England, settings follow the EYFS. Adults also look at how children are progressing in the seven areas of learning and development that are in the EYFS.

Using milestones and also the EYFS framework, adults will assess whether a child needs more support. In some cases a child may need an early intervention. The term 'early intervention' is used when a special activity or way of working is needed to help the child make progress. Sometimes an early intervention might be suggested or carried out by another professional such as a physiotherapist.

Plan

The planning part of the cycle is about deciding what needs to happen next. The adults will agree and then record what the child needs. Here are some examples of what might be agreed.

Additional resources

It might be decided that certain resources should be put out. For example, brushes of different sizes might be put out for a child who is enjoying painting.

Specific activities

Specific activities might be organised for a child or group of children. For example, an adult might make soup with a group of children to encourage them to eat more vegetables.

Change in routine

As a result of observing and assessing, adults may plan to change the routine. For example, a toddler who has tantrums because of tiredness may be encouraged to have an earlier nap.

Referral to another professional

Where a child is assessed as needing extra help, the plan might be to make a referral to another professional, for example, a speech and language therapist or educational psychologist.

How practitioners will provide support or early intervention

As a result of observing and assessing a child, there might be plans as to when and how the practitioner will help the child. For example, it might be agreed that a child needs more support with playing with others, and that a practitioner will be on hand when the child is with others.

Implement

The next step of the planning cycle is to put the plan into practice. This may mean sharing it with other professionals, parents or carers. As the plan is implemented, adults will also record what actions or steps have been taken.

9 Planning in early years childcare

Review

The final stage of the planning cycle is to review how the plan is working. The starting point for the review is to observe how much children's needs and interests have been met. Practitioners might then make some small adjustments to the plan.

During the review stage, parents/carers and professionals might comment and share what they have noticed. When this happens, it is an example of partnership working.

The review stage is also a time for adults to reflect on how well they have responded to the child and what they could have done differently.

> **Exam-style question**
>
> 3 Identify the five stages of the planning cycle. Give an explanation of each stage.

How the planning cycle contributes to formative and summative assessment

One of the most important steps of the planning cycle is for adults to observe children. This in turn means that the information that they learn can be used for both formative and summative assessment.

See Unit 8 for more information on formative and summative assessment, but remember:

- Formative assessment is the ongoing assessment of the child.
- Summative assessment is a 'summing' up of the child's knowledge and skills.

By using the planning cycle, adults can make a formative assessment of children's ongoing progress. They can also reflect on observations that have taken place in previous planning cycles to create a summative assessment.

> **Read and write**
>
> Create a poster that provides information about planning in the early years. Your poster should include information about the importance of planning as well as the planning cycle.

NCFE CACHE Level 1/2 Technical Award in Child Development and Care

Activity

Visit an early years setting or talk to an early years practitioner.
- Find out how they use observations as part of their planning cycle.
- Do they use the planning cycle to plan for individual children or for groups of children?
- How often do they use the planning cycle?

Test your knowledge

1. What is meant by a child-centred approach to play?
2. Give an example of how a setting could show a child-centred approach.
3. How might the planning cycle identify a child's developmental needs?
4. How can partnership working be supported by the planning cycle?
5. Identify the five stages of the planning cycle.
6. Explain how the planning cycle can support a child's development.
7. Why is reflection an important part of the planning cycle?
8. Why does the planning cycle need to be continuous?
9. Why is it important to assess children's development against milestones as part of the planning cycle?
10. Explain how the planning cycle might be used in the referral process.

Assignment practice

Case study
During a radio phone-in about different jobs, a caller said, 'Working with children is easy. All you have to do is play with them.' This has attracted lots of comment on social media. The radio show is planning another phone-in about working with children. You have been asked to call in and provide information about how practitioners plan.

Task

1. To prepare for this call, collect information about:
   - why practitioners plan for children
   - the stages of the planning cycle
   - how the planning cycle supports the needs and interests of children.

2. You have been warned that the radio host is likely to ask questions that you will need to answer. Prepare answers that could be used if any of these questions are asked:
   - 'Surely children can just get out toys for themselves. Can't they?'
   - 'Isn't planning just a waste of everyone's time?'
   - 'Parents and carers just want their children to be happy. Why should adults waste their time on paperwork?'

GLOSSARY

Accident: an unintended incident which might cause physical injury to a child, visitor or member of staff.

ADHD: attention deficit hyperactivity disorder, a condition which affects behaviour and makes it difficult to concentrate.

Adult-led: activities or play that is organised and led by adults.

Asymmetric tonic neck: a reflex where if the baby's head is turned to one side, the knee and arm on the other side bend.

Bereavement: when a close family member or friend dies.

Bilingual: speaking two languages.

Breach: failing to keep to an agreement.

Child-centred: putting the needs of the child first and encouraging them to be independent.

Child-centred approach: when adults focus on what children need and want.

Chronic illness: a long-term health problem.

Cognitive skills: relating to the development of thinking and remembering.

Commentary: talking about what is happening as it takes place.

Confidentiality: making sure that private information about children and their families is kept private.

Consent: permission to do something.

Consistently: for settings, this means everyone working to an agreed set of ideas.

Cruising: how babies move, walking by holding onto furniture.

Cultural identity: shared cultural characteristics, such as language, religion, festivals, music and food.

Deficiency: a lack of one or more nutrients which may cause problems with growth and development.

Degenerative: health conditions that reduce how much a child can do or learn over time.

Disclosure: making information known to others.

Diversity: the range of values, attitudes, cultures and beliefs held by different people.

DSL: designated safeguarding lead – the person in the setting who is responsible for monitoring and acting on safeguarding concerns.

Early Learning Goals: targets for the skills and knowledge that children should have developed by the end of the reception year (Early Years Foundation Stage profile).

Early Years Foundation Stage (EYFS): this sets out the requirements for children's learning and development from birth to five years.

Eczema: a skin condition causing the skin to be dry and itchy.

Education, Health and Care Plan (EHCP): a document which outlines the support a child or young person needs to meet their potential while they are in the education system and up to the age of 25.

Eligibility and admissions criteria: the rules set down by an organisation about which children or families can attend the setting.

Emergency: a life-threatening situation or one which may pose immediate risk.

Emotional needs: conditions which need to be met to feel happy and fulfilled.

Emotional wellbeing: positive emotional state.

Empathise: to see a situation from someone else's point of view.

Empathy: being able to understand another person's feelings.

English as an additional language (EAL): when someone speaks English but it is not their first language.

Environmental influences: aspects of a child's life that will affect their development.

Equality: individuals are treated in the same way.

Equity: ensuring that each child has the resources they need to succeed.

Facilitate: organising the play environment to encourage learning.

Glossary

Facilities: places or equipment that an early years setting can offer.

Fine motor skills: co-ordination of small muscles, precise movements and hand–eye co-ordination.

Genetic make-up: chromosomes and genes that contain information to make cells.

Gross motor skills: skills that involve the large muscles of the arms, legs and torso.

Hazard: something in the setting that could cause harm.

Hierarchy: placing items of a list in the order of importance.

Holistic care: overall care of the child, valuing each area as important and interconnected. In this context, viewing the child as a whole person.

Holistic development: children's overall development.

Incident: an event which might cause an injury or develop into an emergency.

Inclusion: every child is given equal access to education and care.

Inclusive: something which is open to and includes everyone.

Induction: the process of introducing new staff to the setting.

Inherited characteristics: features that can be traced back to a child's biological family.

Intervention: resources or support to help a child with their learning or development.

Intimate care: when taking care of another person's personal care needs, for example when helping them to go to the toilet.

Key person: a named member of early years staff who works with a specific group of children and their families.

Long-term plans: topic plans which are set out over a year.

Malpractice: failing to carry out professional duties.

Media: the way in which types of art are expressed, for example through paint, drawing or music.

Medium-term plans: termly or half-termly plans.

Milestones: skills that are expected at different ages.

Notifiable disease: a disease which needs to be reported by law to the authorities.

Objective observation: the observation is based on facts.

Open-ended talk: questions and conversations which encourage the other person to answer fully, rather than just replying 'yes' or 'no'.

Open question: a question that does not have a 'Yes' or 'No' answer and which encourages children to explain their understanding.

Partnership working: different services and professionals working together with other teams or people to meet the child's and/or family's needs.

Personal protective equipment (PPE): protective equipment that is worn to stop contamination, for protection when dealing with personal care, such as nappy changing and when cleaning up bodily fluids.

Physiological: the way in which living things work or function.

Policies: statements about how an early years setting will prevent or deal with different circumstances.

Potential: what you are capable of.

Primitive reflexes: movements that newborns automatically make.

Privileged information: information which should only be given to authorised people.

Procedures: detailed information about how a policy will be put into action.

Professional boundaries: the limit of a relationship in a professional situation.

Psychological: a condition that relates to the mind.

Ratified: to be formally agreed by government.

Ratio of staff to children: the proportion of staff to the number of children.

Reasonable adjustment: removing barriers and putting measures in place so that an individual can take part in an activity.

Regression: when a child's development goes back to an earlier stage.

Glossary

Regulation: rules made by an authority to control the way something is done.

Resilience: the ability to cope with setbacks and problems.

Respite: having a break from caring.

Risk: the chance, whether high or low, that someone could be harmed by a hazard.

Risk assessment: a check for potential risks so that steps may be put in place to control them.

Safeguarding: the way in which we protect children and keep them from harm.

Scaffold learning: providing support for learning through breaking it into small steps.

Scented dough: a type of playdough with an added smell or scent, such as lavender.

Self-care skills: skills that make children independent, such as dressing, feeding and toileting.

Self-regulate: to be able to manage your own emotions.

Short-term plans: plans for a week or a day.

Spatial awareness: knowing where your body is in relation to things around you.

Special educational needs and disabilities (SEND): a learning need or disability which means that special support is needed to help a child or young person as part of inclusion.

Standardisation: creating standards for all settings.

Statutory: something that is required by law.

Subjective observation: the observation is based on opinions and personal views.

Sustained shared thinking: an activity in which two people, usually an adult and child, work together to solve a problem.

Transition: the change from one stage, place or person to another.

Visual cues: clues to help pass on messages or information, such as pointing to something as you are talking about it.

Voluntary provision: not profit-making as the aim of the organisation is to support families.

Wellbeing: how healthy and happy a person feels.

Whistleblowing: when someone in an organisation reports malpractice or wrongdoing, sometimes to authorities outside of the setting.

INDEX

abuse 27
    emotional 108–9
    neglect 109–10
    physical 108
    sexual 109
    signs of 108–10
    suspected 110–11
    see also safeguarding
accessibility 75
accidents 86, 97
achievement 50
active listening 129
admissions 75
adult-led activities 77
affection 50
alcohol abuse 27
allergies 85
anti-discriminatory practice 103
assessment 171–2
    formative 153–4, 173
    summative 155, 173
    see also observations
asymmetric tonic neck 14
attachment 32
    insecure 30
attendance (staff) 131–3
baby, new 41
balance 55
behaviour management 64
belonging 47, 50
bereavement 42
bilingualism 105
biological influences 23, 25, 29–31
biting 38
body language 129–30
boundaries 50, 123
care routines 51–3
change see transitions
checklists (observation) 161–2
Childcare Act 2006 91
child-centred approach 40, 56, 144, 164, 165
childminders 73, 137
chromosomes 23
chronic illness 36
city environments 26
cleaning 122
cognitive development 8, 14, 28, 169
commentary 62
communication 127–30
    development 9, 16–17, 169
    and transitions 37
concentration 29, 58
confidence 13, 55, 56

confidentiality 111–14, 123–4
    when to breach 114
continuity of care 163
co-operation 63
co-ordination 55
creative play 56
crèches 72
cruising 12
cultural identity 106
data protection 90–1, 113
death 42
deficiency, in nutrients 32
degenerative conditions 30
depression 26, 30, 38
designated safeguarding lead (DSL) 139, 147
development 10
    biological influences 23, 25, 29–31
    cognitive 8, 14, 28, 169
    communication and language 9, 16–17, 37, 56, 169
    environmental influences 24, 26–8, 31–3
    holistic 7, 13, 15, 17, 69
    milestones 10–12, 14–19, 31–2, 161–2, 172
    nature and nurture 22–4
    physical 8, 10–13, 169
    social and emotional 9, 18, 30–1, 37–8, 47, 55, 63, 169
diet 27, 32
dignity 103, 123
disclosure 92, 110
discrimination 87, 88–9, 103
diseases 97
diversity 89, 100, 102–3
divorce 44
dressing 52
drug abuse 27
Duchenne muscular dystrophy 25, 30
early intervention 164, 172
Early Years Foundation Stage (EYFS) 70–1
    areas of learning and development 71
    Early Learning Goals 71
    meeting individual needs and interests 60
    on play 59
    profile 71
    statutory framework 91
eczema 29
Education, Health and Care Plan (EHCP) 149

educational psychologist 149
eligibility 75
emergency procedures 98
emotional abuse 108
emotional development 9, 18, 31, 37–8, 47, 55, 169
emotional needs 104
empathy 50, 64
enabling environments 141
encouragement 62, 141
English as an additional language (EAL) 105–6
environmental influences 24, 26, 31–3
environments see learning environment
equality 88, 100–6
Equality Act 2010 88–9
equipment 95
esteem needs 48
evacuation practices 98
exercise 27, 49
expression, opportunities for 40–1
eye colour 25
family
    circumstances 43
    structure 44
    see also relationships
family support worker 150–1
family tree 43
feelings 57
    see also emotional development
fine motor skills 10–11, 55, 57
first aid 95
food and drink policy 84–5
food hygiene 85, 98–9, 122
formative assessment 153–4, 173
friendships 18
    see also relationships
General Data Protection Regulation (GDPR) 2018 90–1, 113
general practitioner (GP) 150
genes 23, 25
German measles 23
gross motor skills 10–12, 55
hair colour 25
hand-eye co-ordination 58
hand washing 96
hazards 86
health and safety
    equipment 95
    first aid 95
    legislation 83–6
    manual handling 98

Index

notifiable diseases 97
policies and procedures 84–6, 91–2
risk assessment 59, 86, 93–4, 121–2
routines 122
security checks 94
waste disposal 96–7
Health and Safety at Work Act 1974 83
health professionals 150–1
health visitor 150
hierarchy of needs 45–50
holistic development 7, 10, 13, 15, 17, 69
home time 122
hospital visit 42
illness, chronic 36
imaginative play 57
inclusion 64–5, 88–9, 100–6
  barriers to 100–1
independence 11, 64
individual needs and interests 60, 168–9
induction 121
infectious diseases 97
information sharing 162–4
  see also confidentiality
inherited characteristics 23, 25
insecure attachment 30
interventions 155, 164, 172
intimate care 103
job roles 137, 147–50
  see also practitioner
key person 49, 91, 137, 147
language
  bilingualism 105
  development 9, 16–17, 24, 169
  and play 56
  see also communication; English as an additional language (EAL)
learning environment 61, 65
  facilities 77
  planning 168
  risk assessment 59
learning journals 160–1
legislation 81–92
listening 64, 129
malpractice 114
managers 137
manual handling 98
Maslow, A. 45
  see also hierarchy of needs
mealtimes 52–3, 139
memory box 42
mental illness 30
milestones 10
  see also development
mobile phones 124
motor skills 10–12, 52–3, 55, 57
muscular dystrophy 25, 30
nannies 137

narrative observation 161
nature and nurture 22–4
neglect 27, 109–10
new setting 41
non-verbal communication 128–30
notifiable diseases 97
nurseries 73
nursery classes 73
nutrients, deficiency in 32
objective observation 157
observations 141, 152, 171
  four stages of 158–9
  methods of 159–62
  monitoring progress 163
  objective 157
  recordings 160
  sharing information 162–4
  subjective 156
  see also assessment
Ofsted (Office for Standards in Education, Children's Services and Skills) 81
open-ended talk 61–2
open questions 126
paediatrician 150
pain 33
parents
  supporting 69–70
  working in partnership with 142
partnership working 142–6, 170
patience 125
peer support 63
personal hygiene 117
personal protective equipment (PPE) 86, 98
photographs 160
physical abuse 108
physical activity and nutrition co-ordinator (PANCo) 147
physical development 8, 10–13, 169
physical play 54–5
physiological needs 46
physiotherapist 148
piercings 118
planning cycle 166–74
planning documentation 60
play
  activities 54–8
  creative 56
  imaginative 57
  physical 54–5
  planning for 166
  policies and procedures 87–8
  role of practitioner 59–65
  sensory 57–8
policies and procedures 78, 82
  data protection 90–1
  emergency procedures 98
  health and safety 84–6, 91–2

inclusion 88–9, 100–6
safeguarding 87–8, 91–2, 107
see also Early Years Foundation Stage (EYFS)
positive relationships 40
post natal depression 30
poverty 26
practitioner
  appearance 116–20
  behaviour 121–6
  personal hygiene 117
  personal qualities 125–6, 131–4
  positive attitude 125
  role in play 59–65
  role of 137
praise 62
pre-schools 73
primary schools 74
primitive reflexes 14
privacy 113
private sector provision 67
privileged information 112
problem solving 56, 63
professional boundaries 123
progress, monitoring 163
protected characteristics 88–9, 102
provision
  purpose of 68–9
  types of 67–8
  variation in 74–8
  see also settings
psychological needs 50
puberty 24
punctuality 133–4
reasonable adjustments 102, 104
referrals 171, 172
Reggio Emilia 166
regression 36
regulatory authority 80–1
relationships 28, 40, 57, 123
Reporting of Injuries, Diseases and Dangerous Occurrences Regulations (RIDDOR) 2013 86
resilience 38
respect 103, 123, 126, 129
respite 70
rest 52, 53
rights, of children 86
risk 86
risk assessment 59, 86, 93–4, 121–2
room leaders 137
rubella 23
rural environments 26
safeguarding
  designated safeguarding lead (DSL) 139, 147
  disclosure 92, 110
  policies and procedures 87–8, 91–2, 107

Index

suspected abuse 110–11
   see also abuse
safety checks 122
safety needs 46, 49
scaffolding 62
school
   primary 74
   starting 41
   see also settings
security checks 94
self-actualisation 48
self-care 36, 53
self-esteem 48
self-regulation 64
self-reliance 53
sensory play 57–8
separation 44
settings
   absence from 110
   capacity 75
   eligibility and admissions 75
   facilities 77
   policies and procedures 78
   ratios 76, 92, 131
   roles and responsibilities 137–49
   starting new 41
   types of 72–4

visitors 84, 86, 94–5
sexual abuse 109
sleep 52, 53
social care 150–1
social development 9, 18, 47, 55, 63, 169
socialisation 63
social media 124–5
social worker 150–1
socio-economic situation 26
spatial awareness 12
speaking *see* language
special educational needs and disabilities (SEND) 104, 149
special educational needs and disabilities co-ordinator (SENDCo) 147
specialist roles 147–9
staff-child ratios 76, 92, 131
standardisation 80
starting school 41
statutory provision 67
sticky notes 161
stimulation 28
subjective observation 156
summative assessment 155, 173
supervision 138
support strategies 39–44

sustained shared thinking 141
tantrums 18
tattoos 119
teaching assistants 137
teamwork 142
timekeeping 133–4
toileting 52, 53
transitions 33–44, 139
   support strategies 39–44
trust 112
United Nations Convention on the Rights of the Child 1989 86
Universal Credit 69
verbal communication 127–8
video observations 160
visitors, to setting 84, 86, 94–5
voluntary provision 67–8
walking 10, 12–13
   see also physical development
washing routines 52, 53
waste disposal 96–7
weight gain 31
wellbeing 31, 33, 55, 139
whistleblowing 114
working in partnership *see* partnership working